Young Adult Literature and the Digital World

Young Adult Literature and the Digital World

Textual Engagement through Visual Literacy

Edited by Jennifer S. Dail, Shelbie Witte,
and Steven T. Bickmore

ROWMAN & LITTLEFIELD
Lanham • Boulder • New York • London

Published by Rowman & Littlefield
A wholly owned subsidiary of The Rowman & Littlefield Publishing Group, Inc.
4501 Forbes Boulevard, Suite 200, Lanham, Maryland 20706
www.rowman.com

Unit A, Whitacre Mews, 26–34 Stannary Street, London SE11 4AB

British Library Cataloguing in Publication Information Available

Library of Congress Cataloging-in-Publication Data
ISBN 978-1-4758-4082-7 (cloth: alk. paper)
ISBN 978-1-4758-4083-4 (pbk: alk. paper)
ISBN 978-1-4758-4084-1 (electronic)

∞™ The paper used in this publication meets the minimum requirements of American National Standard for Information Sciences—Permanence of Paper for Printed Library Materials, ANSI/NISO Z39.48–1992.

Printed in the United States of America

Contents

Praise for *Young Adult Literature and the Digital World: Textual Engagement through Visual Literacy*

This text will be a valuable source for instruction as it not only introduces digital formats and assignments that may be new for many teachers such as transmedia writing, but also shares fresh and exciting ways to use familiar types of digital media such as Google Maps, YouTube, and Ted Talks. There are also plenty of hyperlinks to online content so teachers can immediately start trying out new ideas!

—**Victor Malo-Juvera**, associate professor,
Department of English, University of
North Carolina Wilmington

Young Adult Literature and the Digital World: Textual Engagements through Visual Media is a much needed text; one that highlights how digital and traditional literary spaces collide, providing teachers a plethora of ideas for guiding their students down a multitude of learning paths. This text provides teaching ideas that will help teachers ignite youth passion, and it will support teachers as they guide students in establishing personal learning trajectories centered on young adult literature and digital media.

—**Hannah R. Gerber**, associate professor of literacy,
Sam Houston State University; president,
International Council of Educational Media

The mobile phones young people carry around with them have more computing power than NASA when astronauts went to the moon in 1969. What it means to be a young adult is undergoing a radical transformation in the 21st century, dizzily perpetuated by the speed, reach, and ubiquity of digital devices. How are teachers to explore that transformation clearheadedly? Dail, Witte, and Bickmore have a way forward. They have invited some of the best voices in the field to escort readers through the worlds of young adult literature and digital literacies. The result is a fantastic collection of pedagogical moonshots that will leave readers gazing anew at the stars with their feet firmly planted on the school ground.

—**Tom Liam Lynch**, professor, Education Technology,
Pace University, creator, Gradgrind's Education Blog

Foreword

When I was contacted to write the foreword for *Young Adult Literature and the Digital World*, I was thrilled to spend some time with the chapters, and—perhaps at some distance—the editors and authors. I have connections here that speak to my experiences, identity, and tendencies, as well as some of my wishes for the future of classrooms and communities.

Centered on young adult literature and its place in society and classrooms, the chapters here speak to my love of young adult books, both to read and enjoy personally, and to engage children, young adults, and adults in alternative spaces, from schools of magic, to dragons, to teenage angst, American history, and more. I keep my own bookshelves and my digital devices stocked full of new and old young adult texts to read and enjoy. In the pages of this book, readers like me will find mention of classic and new examples of literature to sample, with great opportunities to continue to build our own knowledge and our bookshelves.

I have also been an instructor of young adult literature courses for preservice teachers for the past fifteen years, introducing new teachers to the same joys that I experience personally, with the hope that they will, in turn, engage their students in K–12 settings with books that will inflame their own creativity and ideas. Readers who are similarly engaged with preparing the next generation of teachers for public school classrooms will find in this book some exciting and intriguing ideas for working with preservice teachers. For example, Cook and Sams, in chapter 6, provide a framework for helping preservice teachers to compose graphic narratives, a process that educates preservice teachers to "adopt a robust sense of what counts as literacy in school."

Before my work as a teacher educator began, I was a high school English teacher for many years, one who resisted—to the best of my ability—the mandated curriculum that was dictated by the inside of the school book cupboard. Sadly, the book cupboard was limited largely to Shakespeare and classics like Thomas Hardy's *Return of the Native*, Golding's *Lord of the Flies*, and Hawthorne's *The Scarlet Letter*. With my own love of more engaging texts as my guide, I scraped and saved to build a classroom library that would afford my students books that would help them see themselves as readers. If you are like me in this, you will find mentioned not only titles that will engage your students but also concrete suggestions for collaborative and engaging classroom practices that will support you in your work to develop critical thinking skills, a social justice orientation, and a better world.

I was particularly struck by the example provided in chapter 4, in which Crandall and colleagues report on a collaborative project among teachers and their students. They engaged in reading, digital projects, and publication that connected their own lives with de la Peña's *We Were Here*. What strikes me about this student writing is its authentic nature. It is real, it is for a real audience, and it is based on real issues and lives. This is about as far on the other side of the pendulum as you can get from a five-paragraph essay, and it is an exciting approach to community and individual engagement for both students and teachers.

Finally, I am a self-confessed techno-geek. I love new ideas for engaging myself and my students with technological advances, particularly those afforded by multimodality and social media. The book is chock full of such ideas, with particular application to classroom settings. These include Shakespeare mashups, transmedia stories, digital book trailers, and plenty more to build teacher capacity. The chapters here present an engaging and helpful opportunity to build skills and to invest time in new learning experiences for students in our classrooms.

Young Adult Literature and the Digital World speaks to my identity on all of these levels, and I trust that it will provide something for readers of all kinds who are interested in engaging young people with great ideas, books, opportunities, and engagements. Reader, whether you are a K–12 teacher, a teacher educator, an enjoyer of books, a lover of all things digital, you will find some great ideas to think about as well as some practical ideas to use in this book.

The book is divided into three sections, with the sections labeled using the verbs *encounter*, *evaluate*, and *engage*. Apart from appreciating the structure provided here, I appreciate the progressive, forward-pushing ideas inherent in those verbs and that structure. The chapters here prompt us to ask and answer important questions. What are we doing to improve the world, the lives of children and teenagers, and the work of teachers and schools? How are we working together, using the tools at hand, to build a better world for ourselves and our communities? *Young Adult Literature and the Digital World* engages the reader from beginning to end with critical ideas, applicable solutions, and intriguing mashups.

Speaking of mashups, I had hoped to present in this foreword a clever meme, reworked to connect the sections of the book, or perhaps to mesh the chapters here into a single hashtag. I tinkered with some, including #ELAteachersrock, #remixexcellence, and #thewondersoftech. However, my own creativity tends to run in other directions, so I'm not insisting that these particular hashtags will trend. Perhaps I can hope instead to see a new strand of hashtags inspired by the readers of this book, to make the work and ideas of this text more publicly available.

#YALitandtheDigitalWorld

Leslie Rush

Acknowledgments

More thanks than the words can express to my husband Garth for always saying "go for it" when I dive into a project. To all of my students who introduce me to fresh perspectives and invite me into their classrooms, pushing me to do better each semester, thank you.

—Jennifer S. Dail

Heartfelt gratitude to Mike for supporting me, to KT and Tayler for inspiring me, and to all of my students for teaching *me* something every day.

—Shelbie Witte

I would like to thank my wife Dana for her support when I have my nose in a book. I would also like to thank all of my students over the years for their constant inspiration. Finally, a big thank you to colleagues, including classroom teachers and librarians who keep offering one more book to the kids they work with.

—Steven T. Bickmore

Critical Engagements with Literature: Guiding Youth as They Read, Compose, and Participate in the World

Shelbie Witte and Jennifer S. Dail

As teachers and teacher educators in the field of literacy, we often consider whether the work we do alongside our students in the classroom is transferring to students' lives outside of school (Alvermann, 2008; Howell and Reinking, 2014; Moje, 2015). Are the broader skills of reading, writing, listening, and speaking we tout in the classroom being used by our youth to participate in their lives effectively? How can we mentor our youth to use their knowledge to not only participate in the world but to feel ownership of it? How can we encourage our youth to use what they've learned in our shared experiences to not only respect the differences of others but to embrace the differences in ways that challenge the current status quo?

Couple these questions with ways in which literacy and technology interact (Janks, 2012, 2014; Jenkins, 2013; Jenkins, Purushotma, Weigel, Clinton, and Robinson, 2009; Kress, 1999), the increase of youth access to technology (Buckingham, 2013; Li, Snow, and White, 2015; Morrell, 2015), and the increasingly sophisticated and critical ways in which youth interact with and within digital spaces (Garcia and Morrell, 2013; Ito, Matsuda, and Okabe, 2010; Lievrouw, 2011; Norris, 2001; Warschauer, 2003) and begin to see how complex and exciting our work as teachers has become. This book explores these questions as we show how youth learn to interact with young adult literature and digital media in order to engage with and participate in their world.

YOUNG ADULT LITERATURE

By definition, young adult literature's target audience is adolescents (Nilsen and Blasingame, 2012). While we may assign some young adult literature in school, these are the books students will often gravitate toward on their own when allowed choice. And why wouldn't they? The appeal is high, and the texts connect to their lives. The same holds true for digital media. Adolescents are flooded with it on a daily basis and regularly read a variety of digital texts such as websites, YouTube videos, blogs, social media sites, and video games.

These literacies that adolescents naturally engage in often become ignored in school culture; however, it makes sense to engage them with critically examining the ways they read, engage with, and produce a variety of texts—both young adult and digital. Because young adult novels have gained more traction in schools as print-based texts than digital texts, it also makes sense to use them to position students to encounter issues and then use digital media as a means for evaluating and engaging with those issues.

USING DIGITAL TOOLS AND DIGITAL WORLDS AS AFFINITY SPACES

Digital tools abound in our schools and homes. While discrepancies between equitable access to technology and connectivity continue among school districts and even schools in the same school districts, Rideout and Katz (2016) report that nine out of ten U.S. families have access to Internet at home, although 25 percent of those below the median income are likely to have that connectivity through their mobile devices. Given the likelihood of youth having access to digital spaces through their school or home devices, there are limitless opportunities for teachers to leverage unconventional learning spaces, digital spaces, as places for learning.

Unlike traditional classrooms, affinity spaces (Gee, 2005) are informal learning spaces that encourage participants to engage more deeply with topics than they do with the contents of their traditional curriculum. Affinity spaces such as the digital spaces explored in this book offer powerful opportunities for learning as they are supported by common interests and goals, allowing youth to participate in various ways according to their skills and interests, and to acquire new knowledge. In affinity spaces, youth can use their expertise while also tapping the expertise of others, allowing them to work on collaboration skills and developing cultural sensitivities and social skills necessary to better understand the diversities of our world. Through these spaces, youth are empowered to encounter and subsequently produce and distribute texts on their own terms (Morrell, 2008).

ENGAGING WITH AND IN THE WORLD

When we consider engagement with texts, technology, and culture, Jenkins explains that interactivity (Jenkins, 2016) is a property of the technology, while participation is a property of culture. Participatory culture is emerging as the culture absorbs and responds to the explosion of new media technologies that make it possible for average consumers to archive, annotate, appropriate, and recirculate media content in powerful new ways.

Garcia and Morrell (2013) share that while students may be honing complex production skills outside of classrooms, the ways these practices inhabit in school learning vary. The types of participatory practices we can encourage through shared readings and understandings of multimodal texts can shift traditional learning structures in ways that encourage collaborative, interest-driven learning. Through performance, simulation, play, transmediation, and negotiation, participatory culture shifts the focus of literacy from one of individual expression to community involvement.

The new literacies almost all involve social skills developed through collaboration and networking. These skills build on the foundation of traditional literacy, research skills, technical skills, and critical literacy skills taught in the classroom. Janks (2012) shares, "In a peaceful world without the threat of global warming or conflict or war, where everyone has access to education, health care, food and a dignified life, there would still be a need for critical literacy. In a world that is rich with difference, there is still likely to be intolerance and fear of the other" (150).

CRITICAL ENGAGEMENTS AT WORK

Our youth engage with the world through educational, social, and cultural mechanisms in ways that impact their lives, and, in some small part, the world (Jenkins, 2016). When youth take ownership of their learning and ideas, morphing what they know and learn into a deeper or better understanding of the text, they are allowed to encounter, evaluate, and engage in order to explore connections with other texts, other people, and themselves (Turner and Hicks, 2016). This book makes visible the practical ways in which teachers are connecting their students with young adult literature and digital tools in order to engage in meaningful, authentic learning experiences.

This book is organized into three sections addressing the ways in which youth interact with young adult literature in digital spaces. The first section, "Using Young Adult Literature and Digital Spaces to Encounter the World," focuses on the ways teachers use young adult literature as a springboard into digital world, transmediation, and remix.

The second section, "Using Young Adult Literature and Digital Spaces to Evaluate the World," focuses on creating opportunities for youth to express their understanding of what they have read in order to negotiate ways to engage in the world, and, in some cases, to enact change in the world.

The third section, "Using Young Adult Literature and Digital Spaces to Engage in the World," focuses on extending students' work beyond the physical classroom walls to connect with issues outside of their school community. These chapters embrace a participatory culture where students are trying to consciously connect with others beyond the physical walls of the classroom to extend the discourse into a virtual space. Youth are positioned as innovative designers as they begin to create products that present a new perspective on literature (International Society for Technology in Education, 2017). Throughout all of the chapters in this book, youth are the change agents, taking ownership of their learning.

REFERENCES

Alvermann, D. 2008. "Commentary: Why Bother Theorizing Adolescents' Online Literacies for Classroom Practice and Research?" *Journal for Adolescent & Adult Literacy* 52 (1): 8–19. doi:10.1698/JAAL.52.1.2.

Buckingham, D. 2013. *Media Education: Literacy, Learning and Contemporary Culture*. Malden, MA: John Wiley & Sons.

Garcia, A., and E. Morrell. 2013. "City Youth and the Pedagogy of the Participatory Media." *Learning, Media, and Technology* 38 (3): 123–127. doi:10.1080/174398 84.2013.782040.

Gee, J. P. 2005. "Semiotic Social Spaces and Affinity Spaces: From the Age of Mythology to Today's Schools." In *Beyond Communities of Practice: Language, Power, and Social Context*, edited by D. Barton and K. Trusting, 214–232. New York: Cambridge University Press.

Howell, E., and D. Reinking. 2014. "Connecting In and Out-of-School Writing through Digital Tools." In *Handbook of Research on Digital Tools for Writing Instruction in K–12 Settings*, edited by R. S. Anderson and C. Mims, 102–117. Hershey, PA: IGI Global.

International Society for Technology in Education. 2017. *ISTE Standards for Students*. https://www.iste.org/standards/standards/for-students.

Ito, M., M. Matsuda, and D. Okabe. 2010. *Hanging Out, Messing Around, and Geeking Out: Kids, Living and Learning with New Media*. Cambridge, MA: MIT Press.

Janks, H. May 2012. "The Importance of Critical Literacy." *English Teaching: Practice and Critique* 11 (1): 150–163. http://education.waikato.ac.nz/research/files/etpc/files/2012v11n1dial1.pdf

———. 2014. *The importance of critical literacy*. In J. Z. Pandya & J. Ávila, (Eds.), *Moving critical literacies forward: A look at praxis across contexts* (32–44). New York, NY: Routledge.

Jenkins, H. 2016. "Youth Voice, Media, and Political Engagement." In *By Any Media Necessary: The New Youth Activism*, edited by H. Jenkins, S. Shresthova, L. Gamber-Thompson, N. Kligler-Vilenchik, and A. Zimmerman, 1–60. New York: New York University Press.

Jenkins, H., R. Purushotma, M. Weigel, K. Clinton, and A. J. Robison. 2009. *Confronting the Challenges of Participatory Culture: Media Education for the 21st Century*. Cambridge, MA: The MIT Press.

Jenkins, H., and W. Kelley. 2013. *Reading in a Participatory Culture: Remixing "Moby Dick" in the English Classroom*. New York: Teachers College Press.

Kress, G. 1999. "English at the Crossroads: Rethinking Curricula of Communication in the Context of the Turn to the Visual." In *Passions, Pedagogies, and 21st Century Technologies*, edited by C. L. Selfe and G. E. Hawisher, 66–88. Urbana, IL: National Council of Teachers of English.

Li, J., C. Snow, and C. White. 2015. "Urban Adolescent Students and Technology: Access, Use and Interest in Learning Language and Literacy." *Innovation in Language Learning and Teaching* 9 (2): 143–162.

Lievrouw, L. 2011. *Alternative and Activist New Media*. Malden, MA: Polity Press.

Moje, E. B. 2015. "Youth cultures, literacies, and identities in and out of school." In *Handbook of research on teaching literacy through the communicative and visual arts: Volume II*, edited by J. Flood, S. B. Heath, and D. Lapp, 207–219. New York: Routledge.

Morrell, E. 2008. *Critical Literacy and Urban Youth: Pedagogies of Access, Dissent, and Liberation*. New York: Routledge.

Morrell, E. 2015. *Critical Literacy and Urban Youth: Pedagogies of Access, Dissent, and Liberation*. New York: Routledge.

Nilsen, A. P., and J. Blasingame. 2012. *Literature for Today's Young Adults*. New York: Pearson.

Norris, P. 2001. *Digital Divide: Civic Engagement, Information Poverty, and the Internet Worldwide*. Cambridge: Cambridge University Press.

Rideout, V. J., and V. S. Katz. 2016. *Opportunity for All? Technology and Learning in Lower-Income Families: A Report of the Families and Media Project*. New York: The Joan Ganz Cooney Center at Sesame Workshop.

Turner, K. H., and T. Hicks. 2016. *Argument in the Real World: Teaching Adolescents to Read and Write Digital Texts*. Portsmouth, NH: Heinemann.

Warschauer, M. 2003. "Demystifying the Digital Divide." *Scientific American* 289 (2): 42–47.

Part I

USING YOUNG ADULT LITERATURE AND DIGITAL SPACES TO ENCOUNTER THE WORLD

Chapter 1

Emojis 👀, #Hashtags, and Texting 📱, Oh My!: Remixing Shakespeare in the ELA Classroom

Michelle M. Falter and Crystal L. Beach

We either begin where they are, or we leave them behind.

—Hise (1972, 903)

Children all over the United States may have fond memories of receiving and reading the magazine *Highlights* in the mail. One of the sections in this magazine was a story in the form of a rebus, or pictogram, which used pictures to represent or allude to all or parts of words (e.g., http://www.educationworld. com/a_lesson/worksheets/Highlights/pdfs/highlights001b.pdf). Although rebuses still exist in these magazines, children are also experiencing the intersections of symbols and letters in new digital ways. In particular, text lingo, emojis, and hashtags are all a part of the literacy toolboxes that adolescents are bringing from their social media worlds into the English Language Arts (ELA) classroom. And, this excites us.

As colleagues from literacy and English education, our unique backgrounds complement each other's work in the classroom and in academia. Michelle has been interested in how teachers can use young adult literature to engage students, while Crystal has been interested in how new literacies shape students' identities. Bringing these two fields together, this chapter examines what it means to teach ELA in the twenty-first century by making connections to Shakespeare and today's digital world through the young adult literature series OMG Shakespeare.

The chapter begins by establishing Shakespeare's relevance in this digital world and providing our theoretical perspective of digital literacies and remixing through which we view our work. Then, we dig into OMG Shakespeare series, providing tools and practical methods for understanding how to bridge the past and present in ELA classrooms through remixing with students.

A MIDDLE GROUND: MAKING SHAKESPEARE MODERN

Though adolescents are fully immersed within a digital, participatory culture in their out-of-school practices, these literacies are not fully incorporated within the ELA classroom. In fact, students are still primarily taught through traditional means, reading mostly the same literature that was taught over fifty years ago (Stotsky, Traffas, and Woodworth, 2010), despite an increasing repertoire of quality contemporary, young adult, multimodal, and digital texts available to teachers. Given today's digital media–driven world, the ELA classroom should adapt to the needs of students and the tools that they use in their everyday lives.

Some teachers and scholars argue that Shakespeare is irrelevant to the lives of teens today; others argue that the universal themes and messages of canonical texts stand the test of time and merit continued use.

This debate is missing the point. The problem is not that ELA teachers are still teaching Shakespeare and other classic texts, but that those texts are still taught in traditional ways. There is a middle ground—a bridge between the traditional, canonical text and the digital, multimodal, participatory world of the twenty-first century: Random House's new series called OMG Shakespeare. OMG Shakespeare takes plays to the modern era by remixing them into young adult stories using all the tools of today's digital text-message society.

DIGITAL LITERACY, MULTIMODALITY, AND REMIXING

A digital literacy lens can be used to understand the connections between classics, such as Shakespeare, and the digital world of students. Digital literacy is defined as the ways in which reading and writing occur within digital spaces, such as through social media or other communicative platforms that one chooses to use based on social, political, economic, cultural, or historical reasons. It is important to note that while some view digital literacies as equivalent to "new literacies," we agree with Lankshear and Knobel (2007) in that the tools are new, but the literacy practices are not—they involve reading and writing skills. A discussion on tools and language is valuable, but literacy practice within the digital space is the key to success.

Language use must also include an exploration of the diverse modes of communication and the contexts in which they occur (Jewitt, 2011). This multimodality, or the ways in which people communicate through multiple modes (or language uses), is influenced by the culture(s) around us (Kress and Jewitt, 2008). In fact, adolescents are often creating meaningful texts for themselves and others with new tools that allow them to work with a variety of communicative modes (Alvermann, 2008). Consequently, ELA teachers cannot limit themselves to a text-only mentality within the classroom when considering the literacy practices and subsequent language choices students are using.

A specific way digital literacy practices and multimodality work together is through the use of remix. Remix can be defined as "tak[ing] cultural artifacts and combin[ing] and manipulat[ing] them into new kinds of creative blends" (Knobel and Lankshear, 2008, 22), which includes endless possibilities of mashing together one's work with another to create a new text with a new meaning. While most people might associate remix with their favorite musical artist who mashes old and new rhythms, lyrics, or melodies together, remix can include any multimodal works or combination of image, sound, text, or video, for example.

Considering these notions, and how one might connect them to teaching Shakespeare in the ELA classroom, one can see how the past connects to the present (and future). The OMG Shakespeare series attempts to create this bridge as educators help students make connections to a literary genius, known for his or her creative language uses, and their personal lives both in and out of school.

OMG! IT'S SOCIAL SHAKESPEARE

Within the OMG Shakespeare series are four remixes of Shakespeare's plays—(1) *Romeo and Juliet*; (2) *Macbeth*; (3) *Hamlet*; and (4) *A Midsummer Night's Dream*—that all utilize the affordances of social media and digital tools to adapt the classic tales in modern language (see figure 1.1). For those not familiar with these plays, a very brief synopsis is offered here in relation to the remixed versions.

OMG Shakespeare's first remix is *YOLO Juliet,* the story of young, star-crossed lovers, Romeo and Juliet, retold as a series of texts, voice memos,

Figure 1.1. The four *OMG* text covers.

check-ins, and group chats, between characters with the latest smartphones. The story reminds readers that life is short, that is, You Only Live Once (YOLO), so you better make the most of it no matter how many obstacles stand in the way of true love.

The second text is *Srsly Hamlet*, which remixes the story of Hamlet, the Prince of Denmark, by creating a sassy text-savvy teen who thinks he sees his dead father and is hell-bent on revenge at all costs, even if it leads to the tragic demise of Ophelia and others. The title of this remixed story perfectly captures the paradox that is Hamlet—melodramatic and overly serious—which makes the portrayals both humorous and fitting of a teenager.

Next is *Macbeth #killingit*. This tale tells of Macbeth and Lady Macbeth's overzealous ambition that leads to murder and betrayal, and Macbeth's decline into insanity. This story is told through emojis, notifications, Facebook updates, notes, chat-room screenshots, Foursquare check-ins, and reminders.

The final OMG text is *A Midsummer Night #nofilter*. This is the only Shakespearean comedy of the series; however, all four books seem more humorous and comedic through their remixed young adult formats. The humor in this story, though, is of mistaken identities, star-crossed lovers, and a play within a play, which shines due to clever use of Instagram hashtags, text messages, emojis, conversation boards, Foursquare check-ins, and a Tinder-like app.

Together, these four witty texts hold a lot of potential for bridging the traditional with the digital in a young adult literature package. Yet thinking about how an ELA teacher might begin planning and negotiating the use of social media and twenty-first-century language skills needed to traverse these texts can be tricky. An approach that embraces remixing through text reformulations will lead to greater success in comprehending Shakespeare and also make Shakespeare relevant and engaging to adolescents.

REMIXING SHAKESPEARE THROUGH
TEXT REFORMULATIONS

Each OMG book remixes the traditional text by utilizing common text-messaging heuristics, and other digital tools, to retell the story. These books provide a model of what Beers (2003) calls "text reformulation." Text reformulation generally refers to a postreading strategy where someone takes one genre of text and transforms it into another genre of text; this is similar to remixing (Knobel and Lankshear, 2008).

The benefit of text reformulation is twofold: (1) it "encourages students to talk about the original texts" and (2) it "encourages students to identify main ideas, cause and effect relationships, themes, and main characters while sequencing, generalizing, and making inferences" (Beers, 2003, 160). *YOLO Juliet, Srsly Hamlet, Macbeth #killingit*, and *A Midsummer Night #nofilter* are examples of text reformulation where the authors have translated the genre conventions of a play and turned them into a text message, a tweet, or other social media tool.

In *YOLO Juliet*, the original text of *Romeo and Juliet*, where Romeo enters the Capulet masquerade ball and spots Juliet from across the room, is reformulated from lines in the script with stage directions into a Foursquare-like check-in and Facebook post (see figure 1.2). In *Srsly Hamlet*, the original scene in which several guard soldiers see Hamlet's father's ghost is reformulated by remixing the traditional text by using the conventions of an Instagram picture and hashtag, and text message and emoji conversations between those guards (see figure 1.3).

In *Macbeth #killingit*, the three witches have created a Kingterest board, like Pinterest, and have pinned a picture of a possible cauldron spell. The characters are also group text-messaging each other (see figure 1.4). This version is a text reformulation of the setting/stage directions and the famous spell-casting chant the three witches say. And finally, *A Midsummer Night's Dream* is reformulated in *A Midsummer Night #nofilter* when Titania finds herself smitten with Puck who looks like a donkey. In the remixed version, the conversation upon her awakening from sleep transforms into a Tinder dating profile picture and a Facebook post about her ability to find her dream man (see figure 1.5).

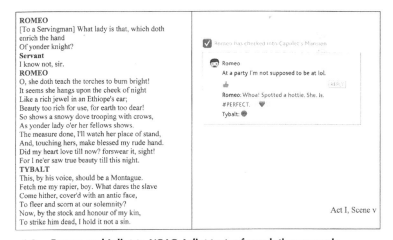

Figure 1.2. Romeo and Juliet to *YOLO Juliet* text reformulation example.

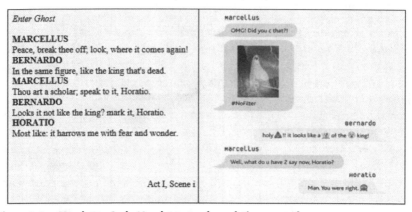

Figure 1.3. Hamlet to *Srsly Hamlet* text reformulation example.

Source: Excerpt(s) from *Srsly Hamlet* by William Shakespeare and Brett Wright, text copyright © 2015 by Penguin Random House LLC. Used by permission of Random House Children's Books, a division of Penguin Random House LLC. All rights reserved.

All four OMG Shakespeare young adult texts provide evidence of text reformulation by using a variety of social media tools and digital language heuristics to retell the tales in a remixed multimodal way. Now that there is an understanding of how remix works within this series, here are three approaches to using these texts in a classroom to bridge the traditional versus digital divide. The first approach a teacher might take is a cross-genre analysis.

Cross-Genre Analysis Approach

In a cross-genre analysis approach, students examine the original Shakespeare text with the OMG Shakespeare text side by side, as shown in figures 1.2 to 1.5. Here, either the teacher or the student chooses a short piece of the original text and compares it to the digital multimodal translation found in OMG Shakespeare. Key to the cross-genre analysis approach is having students determine what is gained or lost in the remixing or reformulation of the scenes chosen. For example, if one looks at the side-by-side comparison of figure 1.3, one might examine the choice of the poo emoji (💩) to emphasize a certain negative emotion. Students might discuss whether this emoji provides an accurate depiction of Bernardo's feelings about seeing a ghost.

As an extension to cross-genre analysis, students could rewrite the original version using their own creative language, emojis, and digital tools. This writing could provide an opportunity for students to compare their analysis

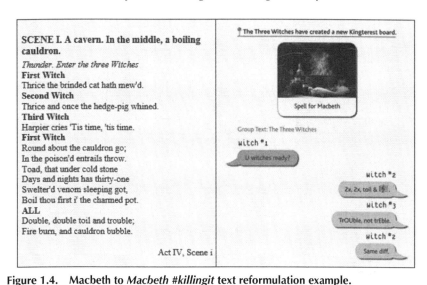

Figure 1.4.   Macbeth to *Macbeth #killingit* text reformulation example.

of the original text with other classmates' interpretations through their own text reformulations, in a gallery-walk-type activity.

Another possibility within this cross-genre analysis approach is to make use of the fact that Shakespeare wrote plays, and they were meant to be acted out. In this activity, a teacher assigns two groups of students to one scene from the play. One group acts out the original Shakespearean text, and the other acts out the OMG version of the text. The rest of the class pays attention to the similarities and differences and then discusses what is lost or gained through the remixed version of the play. Teachers could also discuss how the groups with the OMG version interpreted and acted out the digital heuristics like emojis and Instagram.

A final activity that a teacher might consider doing to help students do a cross-genre analysis across the traditional and digital versions of the Shakespeare stories is to look particularly at the effect of the format on the reader. A teacher could take the scene depicted in figure 1.4, for example, related to the three witches in *Macbeth*, and compare and contrast the original text, the OMG version, a film version, and another young adult (YA) literature adaptation, like *Enter Three Witches* by Caroline B. Cooney (2007), of the scene.

There are many great YA novels that repackage Shakespearean stories in new ways (see Lechter, 2012). For instance, figure 1.6 is a graphic organizer

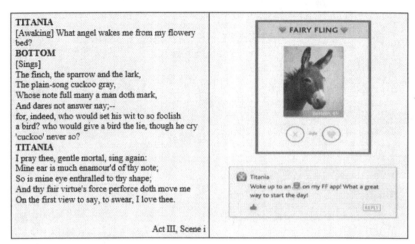

Figure 1.5.   A Midsummer Night's Dream to *A Midsummer Night #nofilter* text refor-mulation example. Excerpt(s) from *A Midsummer Night #nofilter* by William Shake-speare and Brett Wright, text copyright © 2016 by Penguin Random House LLC. Used by permission of Random House Children's Books, a division of Penguin Random House LLC. All rights reserved.

of the witches' scene that asks students to notice what is similar and different across the four formats of text, allowing an even greater opportunity to see how multiple modes of representation affect one's perception of events. This graphic organizer could lead to a discussion of what is emphasized, down-played, or absent in each treatment of the scene.

Mentor-Text Creation Approach

Another way to approach the OMG Shakespeare series is seeing it as a men-tor text for how students might create remixed texts. Here, students would read one of Shakespeare's plays and the OMG Shakespeare young adult equivalent to compare and contrast the language used, as already described in the cross-genre approach. From there, students would combine the overall purpose of the play with the language use of the OMG text (see Box 1.1). For example, students could create their own multimodal literary analysis in the form of a music video.

Through this activity, students are able to create and show a rich under-standing of both texts, the song they have chosen, and how they chose to portray the play. These choices create an opportunity for students to show mastery of reading literature, writing, language, and speaking and listening CCSS domains while also validating the ways in which they are using lan-guage outside of the classroom and beyond words on a page only.

BOX 1.1.   SAMPLE ASSIGNMENT SHEET

Shakespearean Critical Creation Assignment

Over the course of the semester, we have analyzed and have written about all of the texts we have read. However, for this written assignment, we are going to take a different approach: while you will still be writing, you will be writing in a different format. ☺

    Your tasks:

1 Pick a group. You may have no more than three people in your group.
2 Create a music video inspired by Shakespeare, OMG Shakespeare, and a song that you feel connects to the texts. This video should be of approximately four minutes to four minutes thirty seconds (no longer!) and be your group's analysis of the song and the texts.
3 Write a one-page, single-spaced critical analysis describing why your group did what it did; your group needs to include specific, textual evidence from the texts to support your multimodal production and analysis.

Reminders/Notes:

1 If your group needs recording help, please talk with me ASAP!
2 Be creative! You have complete freedom here.
3 Relax. I know this format is a very different type of essay for many of you. However, you are still using the same composition skills that you would use for an in-class essay. Let's talk if you are feeling worried.
4 If your group wants to create its own song, then you need to meet with me to discuss your plans. Same expectations on length, content, and so forth.

If you have questions, please ask! ☺

    In their music video production, students actually are relying on and using *intertexuality* as remix, or a literary device. Intertexuality "denotes the way in which texts (any text, not just literature) gain meaning through their referencing or evocation of other texts" (Novak, n.d.). Students, therefore, are weaving together multiple texts in this complex way to show their overall analysis of the play through their remixed music video.

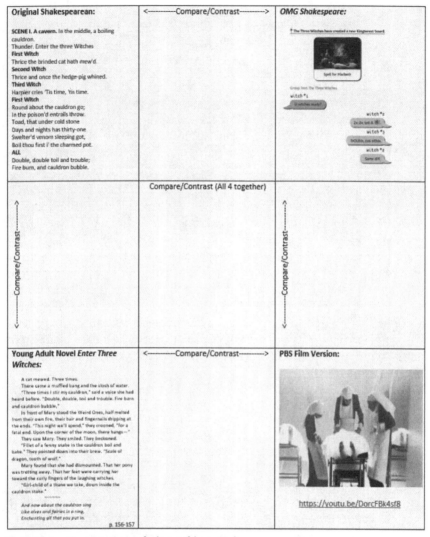

Figure 1.6.   Cross-genre analysis graphic organizer.
Source: Excerpt(s) from *A Midsummer Night #nofilter* by William Shakespeare and Brett Wright, text copyright © 2016 by Penguin Random House LLC. Used by permission of Random House Children's Books, a division of Penguin Random House LLC. All rights reserved.

One of the biggest obstacles for students is that remixing involves stepping outside genres typically assigned in the ELA classroom. While students might feel comfortable remixing texts on their own time through social media, they may associate in-class writing to only mean traditional essays. Remixing texts means that students have complete freedom to create and combine the texts in ways that they feel most effectively show their analysis.

Creating a remixed text brings together the same writing composition skills that are used within a more traditional essay analysis. It is important to remind students that while the format, or outcome, may look different from what they are used to submitting in ELA class, it is actually a lot more complex and requires higher-order thinking skills to create. This, though, is not something to be trepidatious about.

Tool-Driven Application Approach

A third way a teacher can use text reformulation to bridge digital and traditional worlds is by using a tool-driven application approach. Here, a teacher utilizes specific social media digital and language tools within the OMG Shakespeare series as a springboard for an assignment that asks students to take concepts from the plays and write, compose, or produce their knowledge through a new digital modality.

For example, if a class was studying *Romeo and Juliet*, the teacher might ask his or her students to create a diagram using only emojis to capture the changing emotions of a specific character throughout the course of the play. Students could use the OMG book, *YOLO Juliet*, for ideas as to what emojis might be appropriate. Or, if a teacher was exploring the role of sarcasm and irony in *A Midsummer Night's Dream*, he or she might have students create memes with #hashtags related to key humorous moments in the play.

Notably, one of the issues with attempting to bridge ELA traditions into digital realms is the overwhelming feeling that often comes with trying to negotiate the language heuristics and multimodal digital spaces that have evolved with the emergence of social media. Yet one can break these areas down to create a better understanding of them by considering the following: *purpose*, *platform*, and *language use*. Thinking through these three terms in relation to teaching a Shakespeare text will help teachers in that negotiation process.

First, just as with choosing any text, the *purpose* of including digital should be examined. Here, teachers identify the standards they want students to master. This way, the platforms and digital tools complement the work one is already doing within the ELA classroom. Next, teachers consider the *platforms* that will do two things: (1) help them connect to the standards they identified and (2) help them engage with their students. When one becomes more comfortable with connecting the digital realm to the classics, student choice plays a part in the choice of platform. Finally, it is important to identify the multimodal *uses of language* that connect back to the purpose in ways that encourage mastery and creativity. Next (see table 1.1) is breakdown of a few ways one might use these tools with OMG Shakespeare by exploring purpose, platform, and language use.

Table 1.1. Examples of Negotiating Connections between OMG Shakespeare and Digital Literacy Spaces

Purpose	Platform	Language Use	ELA Classroom Activity	Common Core State Standards
To research a current issue and synthesize how it connects to *OMG Shakespeare*	Facebook post, Instagram, Twitter	Emojis, hyperlinks, images, text, hashtags, memes	Students create a presentation in which they research a social justice topic brought up from the text via hashtag.	CCSS.ELA-LITERACY.CCRA.R.9; CCSS.ELA-LITERACY.CCRA.W.7; CCSS.ELA-LITERACY.CCRA.W.8; CCSS.ELA-LITERACY.CCRA.W.9; CCSS.ELA-LITERACY.CCRA.SL.2; CCSS.ELA-LITERACY.CCRA.SL.5
To analyze *OMG Shakespeare* through point of view, theme, etc.	Text messages, Emails, Online instant messaging	Emojis, hyperlinks, images, text, memes	Students create a dialogue between characters in the text using colloquial language.	CCSS.ELA-LITERACY.CCRA.R.2; CCSS.ELA-LITERACY.CCRA.W.3; CCSS.ELA-LITERACY.CCRA.L.3
To analyze characterization in *OMG Shakespeare*	Spotify, Soundcloud, Youtube	Music, mashups, music video, text	Students create a soundtrack of the text (per chapter, by character, etc.) and explain their choices using textual evidence as needed.	CCSS.ELA-LITERACY.CCRA.R.3; CCSS.ELA-LITERACY.CCRA.W.6; CCSS.ELA-LITERACY.CCRA.SL.5

CONCLUSION

ELA teachers can connect the traditional and the digital worlds through any of the three approaches to reformulation, that is, remixing. The OMG Shakespeare young adult series is a bridge for this work to take place in twenty-first-century classrooms. Yet, there are other texts that use a similar remixed approach (see Box 1.2). Rather than abandoning the classics altogether, remixing canonical texts holds great potential for making subject matter relevant. It also acknowledges that teachers and students live in a social, participatory world in which text messaging and other digital tools are an essential part of popular culture and should also be part of schools.

BOX 1.2.   ADDITIONAL REMIXED TEXTS

Aciman, A., & Rensin, E. (2009). *Twitterature: The world's greatest books in twenty tweets or less.* New York, NY: Penguin Group, Inc.

Carbone, C., & Austen, J. (2016). *Darcy swipes left.* OMG Classics. New York, NY: Random House.

Ortberg, M. (2014). *Texts from Jane Eyre: And other conversations with your favorite literary characters.* New York, NY: Henry Holt & Company.

Schmelling, S. (2009). *Ophelia joined the group of maidens who don't float: Classic lit signs on to Facebook.* New York, NY: Penguin Group, Inc.

Wright, B., & Dickens, C. (2016). *Scrooge #worstgiftever.* OMG Classics. New York, NY: Random House.

In 1972, Hise argued for the need to include popular culture in the English classroom stating, "We either begin where they are, or we leave them behind, as we have been doing for the past several years" (903). Although forty-five years has passed since Hise's assertion, this claim—related to the use of digital literacies and popular culture in the ELA classroom—is still relevant today.

Digital literacies like remixing and intertextuality are not new, although they might be new to many teachers. They are instead part of a "new ethos" (Lankshear and Knobel, 2007) that ELA teachers might embody and enact as a way of thinking and doing in the classroom. For teachers and students, OMG Shakespeare bridges the past, present, and future and develops a new digital ethos.

REFERENCES

Alvermann, D. E. 2008. "Why Bother Theorizing Adolescents' Online Literacies for Classroom Practice and Research?" *Journal of Adolescent & Adult Literacy* 52 (1): 8–19.

Beers, K. 2003. *When Kids Can't Read, What Teachers Can Do: A Guide for Teachers, 6–12.* Portsmouth, NH: Heinemann.

Carbone, C., and W. Shakespeare. 2015. *Srsly Hamlet.* OMG Shakespeare. New York: Random House.

———. 2016. *Macbeth #killingit.* OMG Shakespeare. New York: Random House.

Common Core State Standards. *English Language Arts Standards.* http://www.core standards.org/ELA-Literacy/.

Cooney, C. B. (2007). *Enter Three Witches: A Story of Macbeth.* New York: Scholastic Press.

Hise, J. 1972. "In Defense of Popular Culture in the Classroom." *The English Journal* 61 (6): 902–907.

Jewitt, C., ed. 2011. *The Routledge Handbook of Multimodal Analysis.* New York: Routledge.

Knobel, M., and C. Lankshear. 2008. "Remix: The Art and Craft of Endless Hybridization." *Journal of Adolescent & Adult Literacy* 52 (1): 22–33.

Kress, G., and C. Jewitt. 2008. "Introduction." In *Multimodal Literacy*, edited by C. Jewitt and G. Kress, 1–18. New York: Peter Lang.

Lankshear, C., and M. Knobel. 2007. "Sampling 'the New' in New Literacies." In *A New Literacies Sampler*, edited by M. Knobel and C. Lankshear, 1–24. http://every dayliteracies.net/files/NewLiteraciesSampler_2007.pdf.

Lechter, M. 2012. "Old Tales Made New Again: Shakespeare's Place in Young Adult Literature." *English Journal* 101 (5): 88–92.

Novak, S. n.d. "Intertexuality as a Literary Device." *The Write Practice.* http://thewritepractice.com/intertextuality-as-a-literary-device/.

Shakespeare, W. 1979. *A Midsummer Night's Dream.* London: Arden Shakespeare.

———. 1980. *Romeo and Juliet.* London: Arden Shakespeare.

———. 1984. *Macbeth.* London: Arden Shakespeare.

———. 2006. *Hamlet.* London: Arden Shakespeare.

Stotsky, S, J. Traffas, and J. Woodworth. 2010. "Literary Study in Grades 9, 10, and 11: A National Survey." *Forum: A Publication of the ALSCW* 4: 1–75.

Wright, B., and W. Shakespeare. 2015. *YOLO Juliet.* OMG Shakespeare. New York: Random House.

———. 2016. *A Midsummer Night #nofilter.* OMG Shakespeare. New York: Random House.

Chapter 2

When Stories Transcend Books: Ideas for Teaching Transmedia Stories in the ELA Classroom

Rikki Roccanti Overstreet

Our society is at a significant turning point that will redefine how knowledge is produced and stories shared for future generations. What happens in your classrooms is a vital part of the process by which our culture negotiates those changes.

—Clinton, Jenkins, and McWilliams (2013)

English Language Arts (ELA) teachers feel comfortable teaching books. That is what they do, and have always done, in the classroom. Some of them may even feel comfortable incorporating the occasional image or video clip. But what does it mean for the ELA teacher when a story does not end with the last page of a book? How does one teach a story that transcends books and is, instead, a narrative woven through platforms as varied as videos, phone apps, theme parks, video games, and fan fiction?

Such narratives are called transmedia stories and are narratives told over multiple texts and platforms (Jenkins, 2007). The platforms can vary in number from two to, as in the Star Wars Universe, an ever-expanding number. For teachers, the concept of a transmedia story may elicit excitement or caution at jumping on the transmedia bandwagon before it proves staying power. This storytelling form, however, is increasingly popular in young adult literature (YAL), and to address this shift in how we tell stories, teachers need to understand what transmedia stories are, why teachers should use them, and how to implement them into a curriculum.

REEVALUATING THE ENGLISH CURRICULUM FOR THE TWENTY-FIRST-CENTURY READER

English educators are often acutely aware that the reading experiences they cultivate for students rarely resemble adolescents' authentic, out-of-class reading. This issue involves both the texts students read and the literacy practices they employ. Both continuously change with shifts in technology, economics, and the cultural milieu. With such shifts, English education must reevaluate the curriculum, considering how to identify and use adolescents' authentic reading experiences that engage students while simultaneously developing traditional and new literacies.

The twenty-first century is cultivating a generation of adolescent readers with different motivations, preferences, and practices of reading. Modern readers want stories that are immersive, interactive, integrated, and social (Gaskins and Sakaria, 2012, 2013). Transmedia stories provide an avenue for readers to satisfy these cravings for connection, immersion, and active reading. YAL franchise series such as Harry Potter, Hunger Games, and Divergent began with books and then added extensions like websites, movies, social media, and video games allowing readers to connect and continue experiencing the story after reading.

As transmedia stories become more popular forms of adolescent reading, ELA teachers cannot ignore the ways such narratives are changing what and how students read. To leverage these practices and pleasures, ELA teachers must learn how to use these narratives in their classrooms to engage adolescents and develop traditional as well as new literacies while also acknowledging that what and how young adults read are changing.

FROM TRADITIONAL NARRATIVES TO TRANSMEDIA STORIES

The term *transmedia* story comes from the idea of transmedia storytelling, which media scholar Henry Jenkins (2007) described as a process where a large narrative is broken up and parts are accessed through different media platforms. Transmedia stories are the narratives created through this process. As such, they are large, often loose, narratives told over multiple media platforms. These stories are often composed of one primary transmedia text with all other texts considered extension texts of the primary text (Jenkins, 2007). In the case of many young adult transmedia stories, the primary text is a single book or book series.

Transmedia stories differ from traditional literature in several ways. First, they often comprise both old media (books) and new media (websites and social media). In modern YA transmedia stories, storytellers rely on digital technologies and the Internet to disseminate narratives (Roccanti and Garland, 2015). Because of this reliance on new media, adolescents can now engage with transmedia stories through often ubiquitous access to extension texts and by creating and publishing their own extension texts through the use of Web 2.0 technologies.

Transmedia stories are multimodal in that they use multiple modes to communicate various aspects of the story. Some transmedia extension texts are themselves multimodal, but additionally the entire transmedia story is multi-modal since it exists in various media platforms. For instance, the Harry Potter transmedia story includes, in part, books, movies, video games, websites, theme parks, and merchandizing.

In addition to existing in multiple modes, transmedia stories differ in their narrative structure from many single-text stories. Rather than relying on the traditional Western narrative structure in which a story moves from exposition through the climax and ends with denouement, transmedia stories have an open and non-linear structure that does not always end with denouement (Roccanti and Garland, 2015). Instead of ending the narrative with a sense of closure, transmedia stories leave gaps and openings in the text, which allow room for other extension texts (Jenkins, 2007). In this way, transmedia stories encourage continual expansion.

Lastly, transmedia stories differ from traditional narratives in that they encourage participatory practices (Lamb, 2011; Roccanti and Garland, 2015). Through the open narrative structure of the story and the use of Web 2.0 platforms, transmedia stories encourage active readers who engage with the transmedia text and participate in the storytelling process through playing games, sharing content, participating in forums and wikis, and creating their own extension texts to continue the story.

TRANSMEDIA STORIES IN THE ELA CLASSROOM

While transmedia stories can be a powerful tool to engage students, promote learning, and create lifelong readers, educators must learn when and how to use such stories in the classroom as they might not be appropriate and effective in every situation. Unfortunately, not much empirical research has been conducted to answer questions such as how transmedia stories can be used in English education and what the benefits might be.

Scholarship in this area has mostly theorized that such stories promote literary comprehension and analysis (Curwood, 2013; Weaver, 2015; Witte, Rybakova, and Kollar, 2015), develop students' media literacy (Weaver 2015), and encourage twenty-first-century literacies (Conner-Zachocki, 2015; Roccanti and Garland, 2015; Witte, Rybakova, and Kollar, 2015). As this scholarship suggests, transmedia narratives have the potential to satisfy educational standards related to reading literature and writing as well as standards related to media literacy and twenty-first-century literacies.

IDEAS FOR IMPLEMENTING TRANSMEDIA STORIES

While transmedia narratives hold much potential in terms of developing students' multiliteracies, educators must be mindful of which transmedia stories they select, which areas and platforms of the story students read, the assignments and projects used, and how the text and assignments scaffold in the curriculum to support students' engagement with the story. By thoughtfully considering these questions when implementing transmedia stories, educators can optimize the benefits of such narratives.

Transmedia stories come in many shapes and sizes. When selecting which story to use in the classroom, one way to differentiate between the large varieties of structures within the realm of transmedia storytelling is to categorize these differences into four different types of stories: commercial transmedia, franchise transmedia, transmedia from classic texts, and fan-driven transmedia. Table 2.1 provides an overview of these story-type differences in regard to purpose, authorship, and structure.

Table 2.1. Transmedia Story Types

Transmedia Story Type	Purpose	Authorship	Structure	Examples
Commercial Transmedia	To create a cross-platform story that generates profit	Usually a single author or publisher	Usually consists of only a few extension texts	Scholastic's Infinity Ring Penguin Random House's Voyager
Franchise Transmedia	To create a cross-platform, profit-generating franchise for a successful text or series	Usually multiple authors/creators bound by a licensing agreement	Usually consists of many extension texts	Harry Potter series Hunger Games series Divergent series
Transmedia from Classic Texts	To create adaptations and extensions of canonical literature for profit, education, or pleasure	Usually multiple authors/creators without a unified purpose, vision, or agenda	Usually consists of many, loosely connected extension texts that focus heavily on adaptation	*Pride and Prejudice* transmedia extensions such as the vlog series *The Lizzie Bennet Diaries* and *Pride and Prejudice*, the graphic novel from Marvel
Fan-Driven Transmedia	To create fan fiction for a text motivated by pleasure rather than profit	Usually many authors/creators who identify as readers/fans, not professionals	Usually consists of many, loosely connected extension texts	The gallery of reader-created content for Inanimate Alice (http://inanimatealice.info/create/)

Commercial transmedia narratives are for-profit stories initially conceived of as cross-platform narratives. In contrast, franchise transmedia stories are multiplatform franchises built after the initial success of a particular text. Transmedia stories from classic texts are similar in that extension texts are created because of the popularity of a classic text, but these stories are not usually controlled by a licensing agreement and tend to resemble adaptations more than extensions.

Last, some transmedia stories are largely fan-driven in that the extension texts are not-for-profit texts created by readers rather than professionals. Each of these transmedia story types can be used in the classroom and should be selected in conjunction with learning goals, the needs of students, and available resources.

When selecting one of these transmedia story types and a specific story, ELA teachers should consider criteria such as story content, authorship, reading level, size and structure of the narrative, artistic quality, cultural contribution, access to extension texts, and the economics involved. Most ELA teachers are well versed in considering criteria such as story content, authorship, and reading level, but story size, structure, access, and economics may be new criteria for text selection.

In general, franchise transmedia stories are the largest narratives and require thoughtful selection of which extension texts to incorporate, while commercial transmedia stories are smaller and could likely be incorporated in their entirety. Transmedia narratives created from classic texts can vary in size but are often less unified than commercial transmedia. However, these texts are more easily integrated into a traditional curriculum in conjunction with a canonical text. Fan-driven transmedia can serve as mentor texts for students but requires strict evaluation before including them since most are created by fans and are self-published.

Access and economics are also important criteria to consider since transmedia extensions are often created for economic gain even if they are valuable to readers. Some of the mobile apps associated with transmedia stories must be purchased to access content, and at times readers must create accounts in order to access story content. Teachers may want to inquire about their school paying for story content or only use transmedia stories with free extension texts so that all students have equal access to story content.

In addition to size, access, and economics, teachers should select stories they find of artistic and cultural value as well as stories their students will find of value. While transmedia stories can be powerful tools to engage students and develop adolescent literacies, only thoughtfully selected stories will interest and motivate students. To help educators select an effective story for their class, table 2.2 lists several examples of commercial transmedia stories based on grade-level appropriateness.

After selecting the right story for a classroom, educators can use various assignments and projects to help students effectively engage with the story

Table 2.2. Examples of Commercial Transmedia Stories by Grade Level

Grade Level	Transmedia Story	Description
6	Voyager series (2015) from Penguin Random House	A multiple author and multiple platform series about a group of four kids who go on adventures to find a new power source for earth. Includes a book series, videos, games, website, quiz, and special codes.
6–7	The Land of Elyon series (2005) by Patrick Carman	A fantasy book series about a twelve-year-old girl who lives in a walled city and wants to find out what lies beyond the walls. Includes online activities and games.
6–8	Infinity Ring series (2011) from Scholastic	Three kids use a machine to travel back to different places in time to fix the past after a secret society makes changes to history. This story includes a book series and online episodes that include games.
6–8	The Atherton series (2007) by Patrick Carman	A dystopian fantasy series about a satellite world and the young boy who discovers this world is collapsing. Includes downloadable content, secret codes, online videos, and an online game. Also includes an educator's website with lesson plans to teach the story.
6–8	Skeleton Creek series (2008) by Patrick Carman	A mystery series about two teens, Ryan and Sarah, who investigate the strange things happening at Skeleton Creek. Ryan's point of view is told through the books, and Sarah's story is told through video blogs online, which can be unlocked with passwords found in the book. Includes fan forums and sites.
6–8	The 39 Clues series (2008) from Scholastic	A multiple author series about two siblings who find clues and go on adventures to different places in history. Includes merchandise, collectible cards, and online games.
6–12	*Inanimate Alice* (2005) by the Bradfield Company	*Inanimate Alice* is a digital novel that follows Alice from age eight to nineteen through five interactive episodes (with other episodes planned), which include text, images, music, movie elements, and games. The episodes increase in length and complexity as Alice grows older. The Bradfield Company has created educational material to assist teachers in teaching this story.
7–10	Mirrorworld series (2010) by Cornelia Funke	Mirrorworld is a secret fantasy world hidden behind a mirror to which Jacob often escapes. The story includes many references to *Grimm's Fairy Tales* and is told through a book series and a mobile app, which includes movie elements, text, and interactive adventures.

Grade Level	Transmedia Story	Description
8–9	Dark Eden series (2011) by Patrick Carman	A mystery series about a group of teens experiencing curious things at an institution meant to cure phobias. The story includes a book series as well as content such as videos, maps, journal entries, and audio diaries that can be experienced through a mobile app.
8–12	*Cathy's Book* (2006) by Sean Stewart and Jordan Weisman	A teenage girl tries to find out why her boyfriend dumped her. Readers follow along on an app and with a packet of evidence included with the book. The story also includes multiple phone numbers readers must call to help solve the mystery.
9–12	The Survivors series (2011) by Amanda Havard	It is a paranormal romance series about a teenage girl with supernatural powers who goes on a journey to find out about her family who survived the Salem Witch Trials. The story includes a book series as well as an app that includes original music, images, maps, and background information.
9–12	*Gift* (2012) by Andrea Buchanan	Trying to fit in at high school, Daisy tries to hide a mysterious power she has to channel electricity. When she tries to help another student in trouble, however, she realizes she might need to unveil her power. Includes a graphic story, journal, and lyrics and video links for music from the book.
12	Girl Heart Boy series (2012) by Ali Cronin	High schooler Sarah thinks she has finally found "The One" but isn't sure if it will last. This story plays out in a book series and vlog episodes and includes a fan-fiction contest. This story includes some mature content.

in a way that promotes literacy development. Table 2.3 outlines several such ideas for assignments. In designing assignments, teachers should think not only about satisfying standards and learning goals but also about how to do this in a way that focuses on adolescents' reading preferences such as immersion, interactivity, and the need for social connection.

One idea for implementation that focuses on developing literacy analysis and media literacy is to select a young adult transmedia story with a book as the primary text. The book can be assigned as reading for the entire class. Then groups of students can either select or be assigned various extension texts to read and compare with the primary text and present their comparison to the class.

Table 2.3.   Transmedia Assignment Ideas

Assignment Idea	Assignment Description	Common Core State Standards Addressed	Resources
Exploring Extension Texts	Research and evaluate the transmedia extension texts for a given primary text, considering what the extensions add to the primary text and how meaning is created through different media formats.	CCSS.ELA-LITERACY.CCRA.R.2 CCSS.ELA-LITERACY.CCRA.R.5 CCSS.ELA-LITERACY.CCRA.R.6 CCSS.ELA-LITERACY.CCRA.R.7 CCSS.ELA-LITERACY.CCRA.R.9 CCSS.ELA-LITERACY-CCRA.W.7	Jenkins and Kelley (2013) Roccanti and Garland (2015)
Mapping Transmedia Stories	Map the transmedia extensions of a classic novel to show how it has been adapted over time, including the ways it may be an adaptation of an earlier text.	CCSS.ELA-LITERACY.CCRA.R.5 CCSS.ELA-LITERACY.CCRA.R.9 CCSS.ELA-LITERACY-CCRA.W.4	Jenkins and Kelley (2013)
Comparing Primary and Extension Texts	Read a primary transmedia text and an extension text to compare and contrast the two narratives, considering what the extension text adds to the narrative.	CCSS.ELA-LITERACY.CCRA.R.2 CCSS.ELA-LITERACY.CCRA.R.6 CCSS.ELA-LITERACY.CCRA.R.7 CCSS.ELA-LITERACY.CCRA.R.9	Roccanti and Garland (2015)
Creating Extension Texts	Write a transmedia extension text in a new medium for a class text. The class text can be either a transmedia story or a nontransmedia story.	CCSS.ELA-LITERACY-CCRA.W.3 CCSS.ELA-LITERACY-CCRA.W.4 CCSS.ELA-LITERACY-CCRA.W.5 CCSS.ELA-LITERACY-CCRA.W.6 CCSS.ELA-LITERACY-CCRA.W.10	Conner-Zachocki (2015) Jenkins and Kelley (2013) Weaver (2015) Witte, Rybakova, and Kollar (2015)

To encourage students to compare the two texts, activities such as reading logs, graphic organizers, and literature circles could be used to help students analyze what the extension texts adds to the primary text. As they compare and contrast both texts, students will build their analytical skills, and, if their extension text is in a different medium than the primary text, they will develop their media literacy as they explore how the narrative is presented differently in each form.

Another way to encourage comprehension and literary analysis as well as writing skills, creativity, and twenty-first-century literacies is to have students create their own transmedia extension text from an assigned class reading. This assignment can be used with a young adult novel or a classic text. Teachers can ask students to think of a gap or hole in the class text that they, as a reader, would like to see filled. Perhaps they would like to see the inclusion of more details in a certain part of the book, or perhaps they would like to see the addition of more diverse characters or hear events from another character's perspective.

Once students have identified what they would like to add to the story, they can select whatever medium they see fit to create and present their extension text. They might use Pinterest to add visuals and details to a specific scene, write a short story to introduce their new character, or use Twitter to express a secondary character's thoughts. As they create their own extension text, students will build their comprehension and analytical skills while using their creativity to develop writing skills and twenty-first-century literacies.

Because of the diverse types of transmedia stories, these narratives fit a variety of classrooms and curricula. If teachers feel crunched for time, students can complete out-of-class projects that explore and evaluate extensions of the canon or create their own extension texts for classic literature. Using transmedia stories in the classrooms does not have to equate to teaching an entire transmedia narrative. Rather, teachers can use the practices of transmedia storytelling and transmedia reading to address the needs of their students, classroom, and school.

CONCLUSION: EVOLVING CURRICULUM FOR EVOLVING STORIES

The ways humans tell and engage with stories have evolved with time, culture, and technology, and transmedia storytelling is one example of such a change in the ways people tell and read stories. As YA transmedia stories grow in popularity, adolescents are beginning to read more and more stories that transcend books and to crave immersive, interactive, and social reading experiences. Bringing transmedia stories into the classroom taps into these changing reading motivations and desires and uses them to provide relevant reading experiences while also acknowledging the changing ways adolescents tell, read, and respond to stories.

REFERENCES

Clinton, K., H. Jenkins, and J. McWilliams. 2013. "New Literacies in an Age of Participatory Culture." In *Reading in a Participatory Culture: Remixing "Moby Dick" in the English Classroom*, edited by H. Jenkins and W. Kelley, 3–23. New York: Teachers College Press.

Conner-Zachocki, J. 2015. "Using the Digital Transmedia Magazine Project to Support Students with 21st-Century Literacies." *Theory into Practice* 54 (2): 86–93. doi:10.1080/00405841.2015.1010835.

Curwood, J. S. 2013. "The Hunger Games: Literature, Literacy, and Online Affinity Spaces." *Language Arts* 90 (6): 417–427.

Gaskins, K., and N. Sakaria. 2012. "The Future of Storytelling: Phase 1 of 2." http://latd.com/blog/audiences-want-study-uncovers-possible-futures-storytelling/.

———. 2013. "The Future of Storytelling: Phase 2 of 2." http://latd.com/blog/audiences-want-study-uncovers-possible-futures-storytelling/.

Jenkins, H. March 22, 2007. "Transmedia Storytelling 101" [Blog Post]. http://henryjenkins.org/2007/03/transmedia_storytelling_101.html.

Jenkins, H., and W. Kelley, eds. 2013. *Reading in a Participatory Culture: Remixing "Moby Dick" in the English Classroom*. New York: Teachers College Press.

Lamb, A. 2011. "Reading Redefined for a Transmedia Universe." *Learning & Leading with Technology* 39 (3): 12–17.

Roccanti, R., and K. Garland. 2015. "21st Century Narratives: Using Transmedia Storytelling in the Language Arts Classroom." *SIGNAL* 38 (1): 16–21.

Weaver, T. 2015. "Blurred Lines and Transmedia Storytelling: Developing Readers and Writers through Exploring Shared Storyworlds." *SIGNAL* 38 (1): 23–26.

Witte, S., K. Rybakova, and C. Kollar. 2015. "Framing Transmedia: Pre-service Teachers' Transmedia Interactions with Young Adult Literature Narratives." *SIGNAL* 38 (1): 27–33.

Chapter 3

Book Clubs to Book Trailers: Remixing Reader Response with Digital, Mobile, and Multimodal Literacies

Lesley Roessing and Julie Warner

> Our book is fun . . . because he really was, like, running through the woods and stuff!
>
> −Jeff, grade 8

The movement and action within the story was what struck one young book club participant about his group's selection as they discussed their young adult (YA) novel. Jeff could envision the main character as a dynamic agent, moving through the spaces of the story, and that made the book "fun." What caused him to analyze the text in these terms was his after-reading synthesis— planning a book trailer of the novel.

Using book trailers (short, visual "teasers" that advertise books to prospective readers) alongside traditional book clubs allows students to move through the spaces of a story and to get kinesthetically involved in their book club selections. When educators employ mobile tools, such as iPads or other tablets, mobile phones, and portable digital cameras, students are able to move through and across multiple physical spaces to reconfigure those spaces for literacy learning.

Creating trailers facilitates engagement with print text in multimodal ways. This is important in contemporary times when print texts compete with digital texts for students' attention and teachers seek rich ways to integrate technology into school spaces for literacy. Book trailers help students develop important new literacies as they adapt monomodal print texts into multimodal compositions comprised of additional modes such as images, sound, and the kineikonic mode of the moving image (Jewitt, 2008, 263).

In addition, composing book trailers allows students to learn about the writing process through authentic and contextualized activity. For example, they learn revision skills through the hands-on process of digital editing. In addition to learning these more traditional revision skills, students gain digital media skills in communicating through multiple modalities, which are increasingly important in an age of rapid technological change (Kress, Jewitt, Ogborn, and Tsatsarelis, 2001; Kress and Van Leeuwen, 2001). Finally, this activity provides students with a purpose for reading (to create the trailers) and an authentic audience for writing—their peers.

THEORETICAL FRAMEWORK

At the heart of this project are mobile technologies for multimodal composing including iPads, mobile phones, and digital cameras. In the United States, smartphone use among teens is nearly universal (Smith, 2013). Phone-based access shapes digital literacy practice primarily by way of the digital keyboard, which makes the typing of long alphabetic texts cumbersome, and the camera, which allows for communicating with images and video, an increasingly popular youth communicative practice (Duggan, 2013). These communicative practices are also characterized by mobility; youth composing with mobile phones do so on the go (Warner, 2016, 2017).

Mobile communicative practices are often the funds of knowledge that students bring to the classroom (Moll, Amanti, Neff, and Gonzalez, 1992) upon which teachers can capitalize to engage students with more traditional literacy skills involving reading comprehension and writing process. Merging book clubs and book trailers allows educators to build on students' existing toolkits to support dynamic text engagement and rich literacy practice.

While attention to the multimodal composing process usually focuses on what is on the screen, readers' response through book trailer creation involves kinesthetic action of students' entire bodies. Embodied literacy practice involves creating original visuals, including photos and videos, for use in students' book trailers, wherein they become wholly involved in their books by acting out pivotal scenes and taking on the personas of key characters (Ehret and Hollett, 2014). Embodied and multimodal literacy allows for deep, multidimensional, and even affective reader response.

PART I: READING IN BOOK CLUBS

Reading in book clubs is an effective strategy for all readers for multiple reasons. The most important reason to include book clubs in the curriculum is that readers comprehend on different reading levels—depending on the text—and have interest in different topics. When an entire class is reading a common novel, teachers cannot meet the diverse needs of an entire class, even when the class is leveled. Even if a class were to all read at the same reading level, improbable as that would be, individual students would not all be attracted to the same types of conflicts, plots, characters, genres, and writing styles.

Books clubs can offer students a choice from five or six different YA novels, depending on the size of the class and the size of the clubs. The teacher can choose books on the same topic, presented in divergent ways on a variety of reading levels, or books on a variety of topics, written in different genres and levels.

Students meet in book clubs with novels they have chosen to read and discussions are occurring simultaneously in all clubs. In a typical classroom discussion of a common text, only one student speaks at a time. Usually barely four to five students take an active part in a whole-classroom discussion, which generally is teacher-led. For the most part, it is reported by teachers that the same students participate in all discussions. Also, teachers not only tend to control the discussion but also take a large part in the discussion.

Since book clubs have fewer participants, more students contribute to individual club discussion, and conversations occur in all clubs, especially since the discussion topics come from the students. The teacher serves merely as a facilitator and does not take part in the book club discussions. However, he or she would wander from club to club, encouraging discussion.

Small-group collaborative reading scaffolds readers from whole-class common reading to independent self-selected (authentic) reading and, in that way, encourages students to become lifelong readers. But, most importantly, participation in book clubs, and in the after-reading presentations of the novel to peers, employs collaboration and social skills necessary for the modern workplace in all fields.

Conducting Book Clubs with Young Adult Literature

After students choose their YA novels to read and establish their book clubs, they meet and, with the teacher's direction, plan their reading schedule and meetings. Teachers may describe or demonstrate book club meeting format and teach students reader response strategies in order that they come to meetings prepared to discuss their reading.

An effective reader response strategy is the double-entry journal in which each reader notes a provocative discussion point; a quote, character, or plot event; a new or interesting vocabulary word; and a question, inference, or prediction (Roessing, 2009, 173). If each reader comes to the meeting with this information, in most cases, lively, stimulating discussions ensue, even if they never cover all members' journal notes. Also, the journals are evidence that the reading is being accomplished, and having students write about texts they read, according to "Writing to Read: Evidence for How Writing Can

Improve Reading," is an effective instructional practice in improving students' reading (Graham and Hebert, 2010, 5).

Ideally, student book clubs meet every other day or at least twice a week for about twenty minutes and discuss their novels. Discussion points can be shared with the entire class especially if the novels, or discussions based on literary lessons, are being shared and compared. The goal of each club is to finish the novels and book club discussions on the same day.

PART II: CREATING BOOK TRAILERS AS AFTER-READING RESPONSE AND TEXT SYNTHESIS

Text synthesis or text reformulation compels readers to return to the text for deeper understanding, analysis, and application by transforming the text into another format and offering it to others. To foster skills in reflective reading, it is important that students are afforded opportunities to return to and interact with the texts they read (Roessing, 2009, 108).

Since the class members are reading different novels, it enriches the reading community for each book club to share novels with not only their classmates but other students in the school's reading community. The book trailer format is particularly beneficial to both the book club and the other students in the school. As Kajder (2008) writes, "This work is not about doing a 'technology project.' It is about using the unique capacities of the technology to provide a different kind of composing space and, more important, a different kind of a product for an invested, real audience." Integrating networked media connects students with audiences for their work outside of their local communities as well.

Analyzing and Deconstructing Models

The first step of any "writing" or creative project is to share exemplars or mentor texts, in this case, mentor book trailers, for students to analyze and deconstruct. There are a variety of book trailers available to serve as models, and the teacher will want to choose at least three or four trailers—a combination of professional and nonprofessional—that demonstrate a variety of elements. Students can view each trailer and make charts of what they notice as the central elements.

For example, in one trailer for the novel *Wonder* by R. J. Palacio, students may notice that the trailer employs the use of actors, narration (in the main character's voice), background music and other sounds, and ends with an image of the book's front cover. Other trailers, such as a trailer for Linda Hunt's novel *Fish in a Tree*, also include music; an image of the cover of the novel—in this case, at the beginning and again at the end; a narrator who is not one of the characters relating the plot and describing the characters; and pictures, rather than actors.

A trailer of Sherman Alexie's novel *The Absolutely True Diary of a Part-Time Indian* includes a song as the only sound device, telling the story through text—phrases from or about the events in the novel—and pictures and photographs. *The Map Trap* book trailer created by Molly Walker includes images and phrases from the book to tell about the plot and themes. A review of a trailer for the picture book *Josephine: The Dazzling Life of Josephine Baker* demonstrates the effect of the use of simply a song, illustrations, and single adjectives.

After viewing a variety of trailers, students should note the following points:

- The employment of actors, scenes, dialogue, and the variations of those elements
- Diverse images—photographs, pictures, illustrations, and the creative blending and combining of the formats
- The varied effects utilized to present the images—fading, breaking apart, and merging
- Disparate types of music, some with lyrics, some professional, and others created specifically for the trailer
- Distinctive ways in which words, phrases, and sentences are employed and included
- The various fonts and uses of font color, size, shape, placement
- Ways which the pacing of the images or actions affects the trailer and its message
- The use of color

Students analyze the different components and their individual and collective influences on mood and message. They may also note that trailers are from two to five minutes and analyze whether the length is effective for each trailer. Did one trailer continue too long? Was one too short for the viewer to learn about the novel?

An analysis would show that all nonprofessional trailers include a reference list at the end. Students will need to become familiar with the applicable fair use laws and citation format, all important research skills.

Creating Book Trailers: Starting with Storyboards

The first step in creating a book trailer is to plan the script. Whether students in book clubs are designing a trailer that contains live action involving actors, narration, and dialogues or constructing a trailer from images, words, and music, or a combination of both, the students need to plan out the sequence of events.

The most effective and efficient way to plan is a storyboard. Storyboards allow students a means of not only planning the linguistic texts in their trailers like dialogue but also getting a sense of what visuals they will want to employ. Storyboarding is a useful jumping-off point but should not be thought of as a binding agreement; book trailer creation, like other forms of writing with digital media, is an iterative process that will allow students to think in new ways that will allow for revision during composition.

As a starting point, the teacher can create and share a storyboard based on one of the trailers employed as a mentor text, demonstrating how the trailer designer may have initiated the scene layouts on a storyboard.

Gathering Media

With digital storytelling projects, students can choose to seek, find, and take advantage of images from the web, create the images themselves, or employ a combination of both. Teachers may decide to have students create their own images to curtail copyright issues and encourage students to conceive of their own media rather than simply search for it. Most students are already proficient with low-level searching such as Google Image searching.

After students have created rough storyboards that could act as roadmaps for image collection, they can harvest their photos and videos for their book trailers. With adult supervision, students can be taken in groups to the school's football field, the gym, the nurse's office, and classrooms, among other physical spaces around the school. Students will begin to reconceptualize the school space as settings for events from their books. Students see the school in new ways and compose with multiple modes by incorporating the school site, their bodies, and found objects.

Book club members can adopt different roles as they create and collect media to use in their book trailers. They need to collaboratively allocate such roles as director, actor, narrator, costume designer, stage director, scriptwriter, artist, set designer, lighting designer, and visionary. Students bring various kinds of knowledge about movie-making. One book club filmed its trailer, and knowing that they were not going to have the audio in the video clip, a student directed, "Just say watermelon!" (Apparently the word "watermelon" can look like anything on video.) Students can employ creativity, problem-solving, and critical thinking skills as they act out scenes from their books.

Students discuss characterization as they approach the embodiment of their characters:

"That's not how a girl cries. Put your hand up to your face, and make your fingers more like this."

"Sit like a man would, not like a boy would."

To create images, students can harness in their digital compositions, teachers may prefer to use digital cameras or the students' own smartphones. iPads can be used as all-in-one video production studios since they have built-in cameras. Using cameras or phones allows for more mobility. Since students may be moving all over the spaces of school, it may be preferable to use separate cameras to gather their photos and to later load into video-editing software programs.

Editing

Once the media is loaded into the teacher's preferred digital editing software, such as iMovie or Microsoft Photo Story 3, students can begin the digital editing process. Using iMovie, they have the option to "Start a New Project" or "Start a New Trailer." The "New Project" option affords total freedom. Trailers are more rigid templates that can be filled in with student media but cannot be otherwise changed. Students can incorporate their own text, pictures, and videos, but they cannot delete or change any structural part of the template such as the number of "slides," and they can't do a voiceover on the "New Trailer" function.

Teachers may notice that some students already have knowledge of photo editing from communicating via their personal smartphones. In one book club, students excitedly told their teachers, "We are editing, cropping, and enhancing!" When asked how they knew how to do that, students responded by describing a number of scenarios in which they had already used mobile technologies to create media:

"I already made a movie. It was in Alaska. I made it as a present."

"My dad has an iPad." "So does mine."

"I've already used iMovie."

With so many levels of proficiency, it is helpful that some students can use templates with iMovie, while those with more skill and familiarity with the program or similar programs can begin from scratch.

Revision

Composing with digital media is a recursive process wherein revision occurs naturally throughout. Students revise continually as they analyze their work and the outcomes of repeated changes they make to their projects. In one book club, revision happened during the process of filming and as students explained, "We can edit that out."

Music

The iMovie app provides eight different "theme music" looping tracks from which students can choose. Other music can be loaded into iMovie using iTunes, and there is a similar mechanism for loading music into other video-editing software. Students should be prompted to choose music that will reflect the theme and tone of their trailers. They can be encouraged to create their own music if no appropriate music exists.

A useful way of scaffolding music selection process is to analyze various song selections. Famous movie scores such as those from *ET: The Extra-Terrestrial, Jurassic Park, Star Wars, Lawrence of Arabia*, or *Psycho* can be deconstructed and discussed to help students to understand the effect of various types of music on their audience.

One book club exclaimed, "We need the Star-Spangled Banner because it's about America if it's gone down the tubes." To create a song that had such effect, the students ended up singing the song into the voiceover function on iMovie, which was in effect quite eerie and apt for their project. Another group brought in a guitar and composed their own original music to accompany their trailer. If groups are editing together in one classroom, headphones are helpful.

Publishing and Sharing

Teachers can, as a final step, provide audiences for students' final projects. For example, teachers can plan a viewing session for students to watch and critique each other's trailers as a class (see figure 3.1). Teachers can also organize viewing sessions for the grade or school. Videos can be hosted online on an intranet system or on YouTube or Vimeo. Another option is to make trailers accessible on a library computer as a means of virtual "book talks" (Chambers, 1985) for students searching for book suggestions, or by attaching a QR code to books in classroom libraries and the school library linked to trailers.

CONCLUSION

Remixing traditional book clubs with young adult literature (YAL) and the book trailer project creates new pathways toward reading response. Students interact with texts for deeper comprehension through digital, mobile, and multimodal literacies. More students are able to engage with print texts through multiple modalities including the visual, aural, linguistic, textual, and spatial with the integration of book trailers into book clubs. The more

Book Clubs & Trailers Project Critique *[Please Print]*

Name (optional) _____

The novel I read was (title) _____ by _____

I read (check one) _____ all, _____ most, _____ only some of my novel because _____

_____

I would recommend this novel to readers who _____

I like reading in book clubs because _____

What worked well for our book club: _____

What didn't work as well: _____

Making the Book Trailer [check at least one] _____ was easy, _____ was challenging, _____ was fun

Most Effective Technique(s) We Used _____

Least Effective Technique(s) We Used _____

Comment about creating trailers: _____

_____

–

_____

–

Critiques of Trailers Viewed: Feel free to add a technique that is not listed below.
words, fonts, colors. questions, pictures, video, music, voice-over, suspense, novel cover, _____

	Most Effective Technique(s) used:	Least Effective
#1:	_____	_____
#2:	_____	_____
#3:	_____	_____
#4:	_____	_____
#5:	_____	_____
#6:	_____	_____
#7:	_____	_____

Figure 3.1.   Book clubs and trailer critique form.

modes that students are afforded for reader response, the more opportunities there are for diverse learners to develop literacy skills, including twenty-first-century literacy skills related to technology.

The book trailer project represents a means of enhancing and perhaps even transforming literacy learning in ways that support the growth of new literacies skills. Important new literacy skills are developed across mobile multimodal spaces rather than in static classroom rows.

As students move through and across spaces, more active, embodied learning practices are supported. Collaboration is encouraged and group dynamics is activated for highly social forms of literacy learning. A mix of mobility and multimodality gives rise to highly imaginative digital media composing processes and moves reading response with young adult literature into new physical and digital spaces.

REFERENCES

Chambers, A. 1985. *Booktalk: Occasional Writing on Literature and Children.* New York: Harper and Row.

Duggan, M. 2013. *Photo and video sharing grow online*, Pew Internet & American Life Project, Oct. 28, 2013, http://www.pewinternet.org/2013/10/28/photo-and-video-sharing-grow-online/, URL accessed March 4, 2018.

Ehret, C., and T. Hollett. 2014. "Embodied Composition in Real Virtualities: Adolescents' Literacy Practices and Felt Experiences Moving with Digital, Mobile Devices in School." *Research in the Teaching of English* 48 (4): 428–52.

Graham, S., and Hebert, M. A. 2010. Writing to read: Evidence for how writing can improve reading. *A Carnegie Corporation Time to Act Report.* Washington, DC: Alliance for Excellent Education.

Jewitt, C. 2008. "Multimodality and Literacy in School Classrooms." *Review of Research in Education* 32: 241–267. doi:10.3102/0091732X07310586.

Kajder, S. 2008. "The Book Trailer: Engaging Teens through Technology." *Educational Leadership* 65 (6). http://www.ascd.org/publications/educational-leadership/mar08/vol65/num06/The-Book-Trailer@-Engaging-Teens-Through-Technologies.aspx.

Kress, G., C. Jewitt, J. Ogborn, and C. Tsatsarelis. 2001. *Multimodal Teaching and Learning: The Rhetorics of the Science Classroom.* London: Continuum Press.

Kress, G., and T. Van Leeuwen. 2001. *Multimodal Discourse: The Modes and Media of Contemporary Communication.* London: Arnold.

Moll, L. C., C. Amanti, D. Neff, and N. Gonzalez. 1992. *Funds of Knowledge for Teaching: Using a Qualitative Approach to Connect Homes and Classrooms.* Mahwah, NJ: Erlbaum.

Roessing, L. 2009. *The Write to Read: Response Journals That Increase Comprehension.* Thousand Oaks, CA: Corwin Press.

Smith, A. 2013. "Technology Adoption by Lower Income Populations." http://www.pewinternet.org/2013/10/08/technology-adoption-by-lower-income-populations/.

Warner, J. 2016. "Adolescents' Dialogic Composing with Mobile Phones." *Journal of Literacy Research* 48 (2): 164–91.

———. 2017. *Adolescents' New Literacies with and through Mobile Phones*. New Literacies and Digital Epistemologies. New York: Peter Lang.

Part II

USING YOUNG ADULT LITERATURE AND DIGITAL SPACES TO EVALUATE THE WORLD

Chapter 4

We Too Are Connecticut: Digital Ubuntu with Matt de la Peña's *We Were Here*

Bryan Ripley Crandall, Kate Bedard,
Paula Fortuna, Kim Herzog, Shaun Mitchell,
Jennifer von Wahlde, and Megan Zabilansky

And me too. I was part of it. We were all our own people but we were one.

—Matt De La Peña, *We Were Here* (2009)

In the summer of 2014, fifteen teachers participating in a National Writing Project Leadership Institute at Fairfield University were invited by Brett Orzechowski, chief executive officer (CEO) of the *CT Mirror*, to write OP-Ed pieces on the state of education in Connecticut. The result was an interactive website called Special Report: Education, Change, and Diversity in Fairfield County (http://projects.ctmirror.org/fairfielded/), where educators representing rural, urban, and suburban districts collaborated with journalists to capture the challenge of achievement gaps in the state.

After the partnership, several teachers desired a replicative way for students representing the spectrum of Connecticut schools to collaboratively write so they, too, could experience the diversity of the region beyond zipcode disparities. *We Too Are Connecticut*, a collaboration uniting over 400 high school writers through the creation of radio plays, blogs, digital maps, and TED Talks, resulted. With a 2015 LRNG Innovators Award and the young adult (YA) novel, *We Were Here* by Matt de la Peña, the multidistrict writing project began.

Connecticut experiences tremendous economic and opportunity disparities in the state, resulting in one of the greatest academic achievement gaps in the nation (Harris and Hussey, 2016; Radelat, 2015). The LRNG collaboration hoped that breaking down interdistrict barriers and creating an opportunity for youth to inspire youth with writing might chisel away at the inequities. *We Too Are Connecticut—Digital Ubuntu* brought several students from urban, rural, and suburban schools together to demonstrate they are more than the test scores that divide them.

EMBRACING UBUNTU AS A THEORETICAL FRAME

During the six-month project, collaborators embraced a South African philosophy of Ubuntu, "I can be me because of who we are together" (Caracciolo and Mungai, 2009; Swanson, 2007). This philosophy provided shared language for students to explore who they were as individuals in relation to larger communities of Connecticut and worked in agreement with Matt de la Peña's belief that "committing in the classroom doesn't mean closing your eyes to real life" (Bartel, 2015). The six-school partnership embraced in- and out-of-school literacies (Hull and Schultz, 2002) that provided unique opportunities for students to write for audiences beyond a teacher.

Students were encouraged to be observant of their everyday life as members of a youth-centered participatory culture (Dyson, 2010; Jenkins, 1992), to see individual lives as "beautiful" (Buehler, 2010), and to offer local commentary about what they stood for in the state of Connecticut. Using writing activity genre research (Russell, 2009) as a theoretical blueprint, collaborators wondered: "How might a multidistrict, digital writing project motivate student voice and engagement? How might expanding writing communities beyond a single school impact written outcomes of individual writers?"

WE WERE HERE WITH DIGITAL WRITING

We Were Here was chosen for its themes of adolescence, identity, community, and belonging. The YA novel initiated dialogue about diversity, as the characters Miquel, Rondel, and Mong represented varying lived experiences. Miguel was ordered to keep a journal as he reflects on his crime: "I know the judge said for me to write in here four times a week, but what's dude want me to do man, make shit up?" (37). His entries grapple with his existence in a complicated world. For these reasons, de la Peña's text assisted teachers in the six schools to ask students, "So, why are you here?" as they encouraged them to write within a variety of digital media.

At the end of the collaboration, students presented workshops on their projects and showcased writing during a Writing Our Lives—Digital Ubuntu conference hosted at Fairfield University. Matt de la Peña, in attendance as the keynote, reflected:

> I've never participated in anything like it. Kids from multiple backgrounds were exchanging email addresses and phone numbers after they presented work

to one another. They bonded as a community of writers. Seeing this exchange made it all come alive. (Personal correspondence, May 23, 2015)

Drawing from the National Writing Project's model of *teachers teaching teachers* (NWP.org), the Writing Our Lives—Digital Ubuntu conference provided a location for students to share, digitally, who they were together.

Participating teachers looked at students' work that resulted as "new writing" (Herrington and Moran, 2009) and chose low, middle, and high exemplars to make a case (Heath and Street, 2008) about the collaboration. Assessing digital writing protocols (Hicks, 2015) were used. Samples of students' work from each school are highlighted in this chapter and, although students wrote in varying districts, they were aware of being part of something larger.

"Wow. All of This Is for Us"

Shaun teaches at an urban high school. He challenged his playwriting/theater class to write one-act plays on what "being here" means in a small, postindustrial, rust-belt city of the northeast. His students' plays became radio shows, a genre from the early 1900s, as they turned them into podcasts. Shaun's students saw *being here* as having cultural representation within a larger society. They also saw *being here* as having full attention in any given moment and being present in a person's life as a guide and support, especially during adolescence—what Mei-Li says to Miguel "is the saddest thing that can happen to a person" (89).

Central High School, in the state's largest city, is surrounded by suburban towns, and is a school that has made tremendous strides in recent years, even recognized on *Newsweek*'s "Beating the Odds List: Top Schools in Low-Income Neighborhoods." Their teachers have to fight a lack of resources, the pervasiveness of violence, and high absenteeism. "Having the chance to work with suburban schools on the project," reflected Shaun, "was an experience my students needed to have. They needed their suburban neighbors to hear their voices. They needed to witness a different culture that was not of their own neighborhoods."

Shaun challenged students at Central High School to write. His students recorded and edited plays with using a microphone and spit guard with GarageBand on a MacBook Air and cast the writing to be digitally performed. He recalled, "The project also made my students feel validated . . . to have their stories heard. They wrote to communicate their worlds to kids at different schools."

One of Shaun's students wrote a script called "Land of Repetition," a radio play that imagined Eric Gardner, Tamir Rice, and Mike Brown in the wake of their deaths. Briana, the author of the piece, explored what it might mean for a young black male to "be here" in America, in the wake of recent shootings. Written two years before #BlackLivesMatter became a national movement, Briana's radio play reminded the teachers how powerful writing is for students, especially when they communicate on themes that resonate across the national landscape. In the radio play, Brianna wrote,

Mike: What happened to walking home peacefully without being harassed. So much for the land of the free (he laughs). Yo, it's more like the land of the whites.

Tamir: Wow. All of this is for us. All the signs and people? All these protests?

Mike: Yeah, it's sad kid. Another killed from this crap.

Racial violence, at the forefront of conversations in Shaun's classroom, became an outlet for Brianna to explore her thinking creatively. The writing transcended socioeconomic boundaries. "All voices matter," explained Shaun. "They're crucial to the success of public schools. Because students wrote for other students, motivation increased." The students created a documentary of the project on YouTube (https://www.youtube.com/watch?v=1FeFnjAPsz0). They also published their radio plays on a YouTube channel online.

The impact of the multidistrict project for Shaun's students was twofold: (1) students used the podcasts as a way to explore a world that matters to them and (2) they were able to carve out a place for themselves in society. His students felt valued among urban, suburban, and rural peers and saw the impact writing had on audiences beyond the project. "This collaboration," reflected Shaun, "made a case on how important it is to mix up my classroom communities to deliver high quality, authentic writing opportunities. My students walked away with a sense of pride and purpose. They realized they left a mark. They were *here*."

"Putting Ourselves on the Map"

Kate, a teacher at another high school in Bridgeport, used the LRNG Innovators Award to support ninth graders to digitally mark their neighborhoods through storytelling and ethnography. Bassick High School, where she teaches, faces many obstacles. Ninety-nine percent of students receive free and reduced lunch, and the building is in a state of disrepair. "If Bridgeport feels forgotten," explained Kate, "then Bassick feels almost nonexistent." Three public housing complexes feed into the demographics of the school.

In order to bolster pride and to help students find intrinsic value in their community and experiences, Kate initiated a neighborhood assignment modeled after Abram Himelstein's Neighborhood Story Project (http://www.

neighborhoodstoryproject.org/about) in New Orleans. She solicited support from memoirist and writer Sonya Huber and guided students to use Google Maps to tag locations that were important to them, essentially creating a story of the neighborhood.

Instead of offering perfunctory descriptions at each location, though, Kate's students composed mini-ethnographies. "Pushing students beyond apathy is a challenge," Kate addressed. "Motivating them to share writing with others is agonizing." She set out to help her students and their communities to be seen in the same way that Rondel explained he wanted to see in *We Were Here*: "So he knows I'm here too, just like other people" (162). The students tagged churches, parks, and the homes of friends on Google Maps. "It became one way for me to support a learning community in my 9th grade English class," she acknowledged.

One of her students, MDK, tagged a local mosque on Google Maps, a few blocks from the high school—a location his classmates didn't know existed. He wrote, "Ever since my younger brother passed away I've enrolled myself for Quran studies. A good Muslim is supposed to pray 5 times a day, every day. I pray only once or twice. . . . I'll get around to praying more often in time."

Kate's participation in the collaboration provided space for students to reflect on where they live and to detail the locations that impacted them the most. "People think Bridgeport is so bad and that we can't do anything," wrote a student, "but they are wrong. We're Connecticut, too. Where we come from matters. We're putting ourselves on the map."

Kate used Lynda Barry's *What It Is* (2008) to inspire students to think about their neighborhoods. Participation in the multidistrict collaboration taught her students they had more to say than they thought. "The locations they targeted," Kate reflected, "had more than one function and they realized how they were both connected and disconnected from classmates through their ethnographies of location." Writing about their neighborhoods for the students at other schools opened them up more, especially at the conference. "It brought their voices into a conversation where they too often are never heard," she explained.

"So Their Voices Can Be Heard"

Jen teaches at Darien High School, an upper-middle-class suburban school with a reputation for academic and athletic excellence. She partnered with Paula, a teacher at Center for Global Studies, an interdistrict magnet school in urban-suburban Norwalk, to support student blogging. Jen was worried that her students were too reliant on external motivation and extrinsic support because of the high pressure placed on them to excel, and she wanted to challenge them to be more comfortable taking risks with their writing. "I set out to encourage a space where my students could engage with books and share ideas beyond hours in a classroom," Jen reflected.

Paula desired the same but recognized that her students, coming from multiple areas of the state, arrived to her classroom receptive to writing in digital platforms. Both teachers wanted students to write in their own voices, to express authentic selves, and to explore how to creatively publish work in a digital format. They also wanted them to shape a positive digital footprint and be responsible for how they represent themselves online.

After reading *The Catcher in the Rye*, Jen's students turned a more critical lens on the community of Darien and, with blogs, found the freedom to critique where they live. Whereas students usually were shy about sharing anything other than positive perspectives about the opportunities and resources of their community, having them write in the voice of Holden Caulfield allowed them to speak more honestly. One of her students reflected, "Teenagers write in social media so they can express their opinions and feelings; so their voices can be heard." Jen's students wrote on their blogs about feeling marginalized, boxed in, and restricted by school, sports, and extracurricular activities.

Like Holden, Jen felt, Miguel shares a similar distrust of an adult world. In *We Were Here* Miguel writes, "*Nothing* matters. Not when you break it all down like I been doing in my head," and continues, "It's all meaningless. Everybody. Is. Nobody" (de la Peña, 284). Reading Holden and Miguel's narratives helped Jen's students to realize that their opinions and voices did matter, especially when she encouraged them to maintain a blog to explore the worlds where they live. One of her students wrote on a classroom blog about his attendance in a camp each summer, an opportunity he took for granted:

> When you live under the same conditions for a long period of time, they become habit or expected. I had become used to all of the hospitality I received daily from my parents to the point where I lost my respect for it. When I went to camp, I had no parent to rely on no matter what, and I had to learn how to live more individually. It built up my work ethic but, more importantly, it made me realize how nice, kind, caring, and hardworking my parents are.

The blog, written in Jen's tenth-grade English class, was a location for students to share narratives about life, to upload photos, and to make connections with the texts read in her class.

In Paula's classroom, students also carved out digital spaces where they blogged on social issues such as gender identity and animal welfare, analyzed song lyrics, reviewed books, and wrote about their relationship to larger communities. The diversity of Paula's students' backgrounds was genuinely reflected in their writing. "I watched my kids develop skill and confidence in writing, as they practiced giving feedback to peers online," Paula reflected. "Digital publishing helped my 9th grade writers to create content with a purpose that went beyond the teacher and an assignment in school."

Paula's students created a directory of over seventy-five blogs that was shared during the Writing Our Lives—Digital Ubuntu conference. The student blogs covered topics such as becoming a pilot and swimming on a Varsity swim team to displaying art portfolios with artistic statements. One of Paula's students maintained an advice blog that encouraged female classmates to take care of themselves. On it, she wrote

> Obviously, you're in high school right now so this is a time where you learn more about yourself. You become the person you are, you experiment and have fun. I feel like everyone feels they need to fit in: wear the same thing, act the same way, and just become the same person. But I say, don't be someone you're not, because it's not worth it in the end. You need to have self-confidence, and be the best person you want to be.

The student writer envisioned an audience of like-minded girls and her entries served to inform and build community. She had purpose with her writing and was motivated to share insights about insecurity and peer pressure.

At the culminating Writing Our Lives—Digital Ubuntu conference, students presented written work and, more importantly, discussed how digital composing united their many communities. "My students left the conference thinking they had the best projects. They were really proud," bragged Jen. "But then I talked to the other teachers who said *their* students said the same thing. All the students thought they did the best work, which is awesome. They were all proud of what they wrote."

"We May Not Have It All Together, but Together We Can Have It All"

Megan teaches at Joel Barlow regional high school, a school nestled in northeast Fairfield County that serves the rural towns of Easton and Redding. She collaborated with Kim, a teacher at Staples High School in Westport, a silver-medal winner in the National Rankings of schools. Together, they worked to support TED Talks and presentation skills.

Barlow and Staples have a reputation for being academically motivated with over 50 percent of students taking AP courses (an average of three tests per student) and high college acceptance rates. Joel Barlow, in fact, operates under the William Butler Yeats' quotation: "Education is not the filling of a pail but the lighting of a fire," with a dedication to support student integrity, intellectual curiosity, and uplifting student voice.

As an English teacher at Barlow, Megan found inspiration from the TED motto: "Ideas worth spreading." In collaboration with Kim, she designed a semester-long project in an elective, Writing to Speak: Words to Be Heard. Themes of the talks were inspired by de la Peña's text *We Were Here* and the "I, Too, Am Harvard" campaign where diverse students made the case that their voices matter, too.

Her students brainstormed outsiders' perceptions, images, and stereotypes of their school's community and its surrounding towns. They evaluated their lists to see what negative stereotypes weren't true (i.e., weren't confirmed in their own life experiences), and where negative stereotypes might be true, but need to be combatted. Between the schools, classes shared drafts of their writing and supported each other's revisions, most notably through a field trip to attend workshops by Robert Galinsky, a Teen TED Talks coach.

In one of the TED Talks, "Exposing Vulnerability," a student named Andrea broke down a stereotypical notion of the "perfect" family in Fairfield County. She shared an emotional, personal struggle with an eating disorder, and made the claim.

> Our interactions and relationships are only real and raw and productive when we are completely representing ourselves. To do this we must be vulnerable. We must step out of our comfort zone and promote the unknown. We must promote an authentic true self-image. True micro moments of connection with others are at their highest when we are absolutely and completely vulnerable with each other.

Andrea concluded the TED Talks performance with a call to action and urged peers to dispel destructive stereotypes and to find strength through sharing obstacles with those around them. It was as if she were following Miguel's advice on writing, "They just tell the whole story, no matter how hard it was to say, because people need to read it" (350). Andrea stated, "We may not have it all together, but together, we can have it all."

She drew on her personal life to enter a national conversation via a subject that mattered to her in order to evoke change. She took a huge risk sharing sensitive, personal information, showing she trusted her peers, and more importantly, like Miguel, saw that her voice was valuable and needed.

Similarly, Kim wanted students' voices to be heard beyond the insularity of their local community, and for them to further engage with academic risks to write for a wider audience. She collaborated with Megan in support of expanding TED Talks in the classroom and to provide a means for establishing more voice in the writing of her students.

One of Kim's students, Deanna, wrote and performed "Life Versus Death: In Reflection," a TED Talk based on her experience as an emergency medical technician (EMT) in Westport, Connecticut. She provided perspective through sharing the average pressure a high school student feels, versus the pressure one feels when faced with a life-or-death situation. Through her work experience, she realized that "being here" meant being present for those who needed her the most in any given moment, even with the pressures students face regarding their futures in southern Connecticut.

Deanna's TED Talk utilized some key features to reinforce her purpose. She opened her talk not directly addressing her audience but with an emergency call that changed her perspective on what it means to be alive. Immediately, the audience was placed in that moment, a key component of effective TED Talks. In sharing her story, both as a former "grade-grubbing" student and with her work as an EMT, Deanna provided pathos and allowed her audience to connect with her and her message on a personal level. She balanced this with ethos, too, giving herself credibility while appealing to her audience's emotions. Deanna wrote:

> Find something that you love and that you're passionate about. . . . I'm asking that all of you who have ever cried or thought of yourself as less valuable because of a bad grade to put it in the past and realize how truly lucky we are.

Through applying rhetorical strategies, Deana's talk became less of a speech and more of a TED Talk through appealing to and involving her audience.

Through this experience, Megan and Kim realized that the biggest rewards from teaching involve some level of risk, and that encouraging students to write for performance was a game changer in their classrooms. If teachers take risks, such as writing for audiences beyond a single classroom, then authentic student learning occurs. Teachers, like students, should be respected as risk takers.

The Writing Our Lives—Digital Ubuntu conference allowed the students to see peers as they presented. They became leaders for underclassmen while they explained how they arrived at topics, how they formulated speeches, and how they developed a final product. The interdistrict, student-led conference enhanced the voices they used through writing. As students watched and listened to the performances—both within their own classrooms and for other presenters—they found themselves uniting with the diversity of Connecticut. They realized that who they are, while they're here, mattered most when they connected with others.

CONCLUSION

While autographing multiple copies of *We Were Here* during the Writing Our Lives—Digital Ubuntu conference, Matt de la Peña inscribed for students,

"Let them know you're here." The intent of our LRNG Innovators Award was to offer students from multiple backgrounds a location to show that their stories matter, too. More importantly, we wanted students to know that individuality—no matter the school attended—is stronger when united in a community of others.

In summary, over 400 young people in southern Connecticut participated in the six-school, interdistrict writing project. All the digital writing—radio plays, ethnographies, blogs, and TED Talks—was saved so teachers could think critically about instructional practices and written outcomes achieved. Through professional work, especially the influence of the National Writing Project, teachers realized the importance of community in support of young writers, especially when helping them to reach a written outcome. The project, united under the Ubuntu philosophy, offered an opportunity for six schools to think critically about their communities and to interact with others.

As Miller (2016) wrote, "We are called to care for each other, to listen to each other's voices, triumphs, tensions, and even pain. We are called together by mutual interests, challenging myriad inequities, shifting educational contexts, and for standing up in the face of adversity" (217). The voice of a single teacher, it was learned, is made stronger when united in collaboration with fellow teachers. Professional work is validated when shared and discussed with one another.

Chapter subheadings demonstrate what was learned through the collaboration. As teachers outlined the project with students—sharing writing tasks, distributing *We Were Here*, and providing technical equipment to support the work—students grew impressed ("Wow. All of This Is for Us). Students appreciated the opportunity to share digital work ("Putting Ourselves on the Map") and to have space to articulate their ideas ("So Their Voices Can Be Heard"). Promoting Ubuntu helped educators achieve the goal of uniting heterogeneous populations of youth ("We may not have it all together, but together we can have it all").

Of equal importance, however, was the contribution of *We Were Here* by Matt de la Peña to the larger mission of the collaboration. Throughout the work, teachers set out to instill ways that writing establishes, unites, and brings about community. The goal was for students to have a similar realization as Miguel when he played in the drum circle and when he found harmony working on the farm: "I was part of it. We were all our own people but we were one" (332).

Community strength comes from the dignity of individuals who are empathetic and generous with support of one another. Teachers realized that putting a dent in Connecticut's achievement gap is a difficult task, but collaborative projects push against ways individual districts are positioned in relationship to each other. Rather than distancing young people through zip code and school divisions, teachers wanted young people to know that as a collective they are Connecticut, too.

Pairing de la Peña's YA novel with the big question "Why are you here?" allowed students to explore thinking through writing. Digital media enhanced the voices and motivated them to write for larger audiences. Throughout the six-month collaboration and during the Writing Our Lives—Digital Ubuntu conference students learned that a person is a person through relationships with others (Swanson, 2007, 54). Writing inspired by de la Peña's text helped the six schools to remix traditional boundaries. In the end, the differences between communities made better bridges for understanding one another. For a little while in Connecticut, we were here, too.

REFERENCES

Barry, L. 2008. *What It Is*. Montreal: Drawn and Quarterly.

Bartel, J. 2015. "One Thing Leads to Another: An Interview with Matt de la Peña." http://www.yalsa.ala.org/thehub/2015/08/06/one-thing-leads-to-another-an-interview-with-matt-de-la-pena/.

Buehler, J. 2010. "'Their Lives Are Beautiful, Too': How Matt de la Pena Illuminates the Lives of Urban Teens." *ALAN Review* 36 (1): 36–43.

Caracciolo, D., and A. M. Mungai, A. M. 2009. *In the Spirit of Ubuntu: Stories of Teaching and Research*. Boston: Sense Publishers.

de la Peña, M. 2010. *We Were Here*. New York: Emblem Press.

Dyson, A. H. 2010. "Opening Curricular Closets in Regulated Times: Finding Pedagogical Keys." *English Education* 42 (3): 307–319.

Harris, E. A., and K. Hussey. 2016. "In Connecticut, a Wealth Gap Divides Neighboring Schools." *New York Times*. September 11, 2016.

Heath, S. B., and B. V. Street. 2008. *On Ethnography: Approaches to Language and Literacy*. New York: Teachers College Press.

Herrington, A., and C. Moran. 2009. *Teaching the New Writing: Technology, Change, and Assessment in the 21st-Century Classroom*. New York: Teachers College Press and National Writing Project.

Hicks, T. 2015. *Assessing Students' Digital Writing*. New York: Teachers College Press and National Writing Project.

Hull, B., and K. Schultz. 2002. *School's Out! Bridging Out-of-School Literacies with Classroom Practice*. New York: Teachers College Press.

Jenkins, H. 1992. *Textual Poachers: Television Fans and Participatory Culture*. New York: Routledge

Miller, S. 2016. "Ubuntu: Calling *in* the Field." *English Education* 48 (3): 192–200.

Radelat, A. July 6, 2015. "Achievement Gap an Issue as Congress Considers New Ed Bill." *CT Mirror*. http://ctmirror.org/2015/07/06/achievement-gap-an-issue-as-congress-considers-new-ed-bill/.

Russell, D. 2009. "Uses of Activity Theory in Written Communication Research." In *Learning and Expanding with Activity Theory*, edited by A. Sannino, H. Daniels, and K. D. Gutiérrez. Cambridge: Cambridge University Press.

Salinger, J. D. 1945. *Catcher in the Rye*. New York: Little, Brown, & Company.

Swanson, D. M. 2007. "Ubuntu: An African Contribution to (Re)search for/with a 'Humble Togetherness'." *Journal of Contemporary Issues in Education* 2 (2): 53–67.

Chapter 5

Becoming a Global and Digital Citizen through the Power of Young Adult Literature

Kathryn Bailey

> Learning occurs within each of us separately, pushed forward by interactions across the lines that divide us.
>
> —Klarke (2013, 20)

In an era emphasizing standardized tests that limit the possibility of creativity, cultural awareness, and exploration of societal issues, it is essential that teachers teach *students* rather than the *test*. Once students graduate, semesters will no longer dictate deadlines, and life will no longer ask students to make decisions based on a, b, or c, with one right answer always in the mix of two wrong. Rather, life will ask these former students to choose a path in which they can be catalysts for positive social change, to choose a path in which they make a difference by serving others rather than simply the status quo, to choose a path in which it is no longer about the destination (the test) but the journey (the learning along the way).

Students are in dire need of educators that are equally hungry, desperate for total immersion in fantastic and life-changing material: books that challenge them to think past self and into the hearts and lives of others, and assessments that ask them to step outside (physically or virtually) the four walls of a classroom. It might be bold, but perhaps the answer is to let teachers take the passenger's seat. Perhaps the answer is to value the lives students bring to school every day. Perhaps the answer is to embrace diversity. And perhaps, to accomplish this, teachers can introduce students to relevant young adult literature (YAL) and ask them to complete authentic, personal assessments.

Kathryn Bailey

STATEMENT OF PROBLEM: IT IS TIME

How can a teacher increase student awareness, participation, and activism in the classroom? How can students better comprehend YAL by exploring real-world issues? The combination of YAL and authentic assessment through engaging discussions, social action research, and problem-based learning is more authentic to the expectations of life after high school than the reading of canonical literature and assessments created for the art of regurgitation.

Another question is, how do teachers not only give voices to those who are marginalized, but, in turn, offer ways to move beyond marginalization? How do teachers not only introduce students to texts and characters that so clearly match their own lives but also equip them with skills to be social advocates for themselves and for others? It is time. It is time to wake up our students. When given the opportunity, they will flourish.

THEORETICAL FRAMEWORK

The following proposed course of action in any middle or high school English Language Arts (ELA) class can be tailored to fit the needs of the teachers and, most importantly, the students. What is outlined next is not only created to introduce the type of classroom experience previously described but also designed to meet the NCTE/IRA Standards for ELA.

Students will not only read but also identify and analyze authentic issues in self-selected young adult texts. They will research, produce multiple genres of writing, and communicate with others via social media to create awareness. They may potentially suggest solutions for the problems in the text as well as in their immediate communities.

WHAT CONVERSATIONS DO YOUR KIDS NEED TO HAVE?

There is an abundance of fantastic YAL on the market right now. Teachers must build solid relationships with their students, communities, parents, and administration to get a feel for not only what is appropriate but also what conversations are *needed* in their classrooms. For instance, a school in a community with gang violence may consider *A Long Way Gone* by Ishmael Beah, a memoir about child soldiers in Sierra Leone. Though this does not discuss the same violence the students in the community may face, it *does* discuss what happens when children are under the influence of powerful and dangerous authority figures.

A school with a bullying epidemic may read *Night*, a Holocaust memoir by Elie Wiesel, which begs readers to consider how silence perpetuates violence, and whether people who stay silent when they witness injustice are equally responsible for its occurrence. These texts do not explicitly and immediately correlate to the exact issues in the community, and this is a good thing. When choosing texts, teachers must truly dig deep and leave that discovery up to the students.

The following books represent a small number of rich texts that deal with various social issues:

- *Whale Talk* by Chris Crutcher (2001): Discusses social identity, cliques, sports, and handicap
- *Twisted* by Laurie Halse Anderson (2007): Discusses integrity, responsibility, and alcohol use
- *Eleanor and Park* by Rainbow Rowell (2013): Discusses diversity, bullying, love, friendship, and family
- *Crank* by Ellen Hopkins (2004): Discusses drug abuse and addiction and personal identity
- *The Fault in Our Stars* by John Green (2012): Discusses cancer, losing loved ones, and coping with loss
- *Swallowing Stones* by Joyce McDonald (1997): Discusses peer pressure, betrayal, and social justice
- *Girls Like Us* by Gail Giles (2014): Discusses bullying, abuse, and exceptional needs

As teachers begin to implement texts like these in their classrooms through whole-group direct instruction, small book clubs, or even independent reading, they then have to consider the most important part of the experience: *how am I going to assess if my students can take the information from the text and implement a beneficial action?*

PRACTICAL METHODS

How a teacher begins a journey to use YAL to promote social changes depends entirely on how he or she plans to have students read these texts. Here are three different ways these books can be read in the classroom:

1 Students choose novels that they will read independently. As students begin digesting their self-selected novels, teachers can have authentic book talks where students discuss the social injustices or issues they discover. As students explore the core questions at the heart of the novel, they

can use those questions to create conversations as jumping-off points for the work that will follow.

2 The whole class can read one novel together. Teachers can facilitate whole-group conversations based on characters and action in the novel that represent the issues their students face every day. Personal connections may work well for younger students. Teachers can ask students to immerse themselves in the lives of the characters to develop empathy and social awareness with every turn of the page. Whole group instruction is also a good way to include instruction on grammar and mechanics, author's purpose, and the power of language and identity through reading.

3 Students can be grouped into small book clubs so that multiple books are read at one time. In this scenario, students help one another, struggle through issues together, and get assistance from the teacher, when needed, throughout the reading. Teachers can consider a literature circle culture in which students have roles to fulfill as they read. For example, a discussion leader writes questions, a quote master documents textual evidence of social (in)justice in the book, and a fact-checker looks up statistics on social issues as they read the novel.

The sky is the limit! The point is to get these students engaging with one another and developing empathy and a thirst for equity as a group. Once they've done this, it is easy to charge them with a call to action.

Next, teachers can consider pairing the YAL with nonfiction texts such as essays, memoirs, documentaries, and current, relevant articles. This approach leads to powerful conversations about real people, and *especially* teenagers, who have made a positive impact on their communities.

Nonfiction texts for consideration include, but are not limited to, the following:

• Essay: *Civil Disobedience* by Henry David Thoreau—discusses social justice, power, and authority
• Documentary: *Hungry for Change* directed by James Colquhoun, Laurentine ten Bosch, Carlo Ledesma—discusses health and wellness, corrupt politics, and business
• Book: *The Rose That Grew from Concrete* by Tupac Shakur (1999)—discusses poverty, loneliness, and fame

It is incredibly powerful to ask students to conduct their own research and find articles to match their books. Once students have made connections between YAL and multiple forms of nonfiction, teachers are ready to introduce ways in which students can show mastery of content/standards in an authentic way. This approach asks students to identify major issues within the texts they have read and choose one for which they are willing to fight.

Students can begin with an annotated bibliography based on valid, academic research on their topics. They can follow up with a researched, argumentative essay about the historical context of their topic and their proposed solution to the problem. Next, teachers can encourage students to take their research further by writing campaign letters to authority figures in the area they are hoping to change. This can be finalized by a defense/speech in which students advocate for their solution in front of a panel of teachers or community leaders (preferably leaders in their field).

To engage students throughout this entire process, teachers can assign writing in the form of a social media campaign. Students can use their research with examples from literature to create a campaign on a social media site like Twitter to raise awareness of their social issue and their proposed solution.

Students create accounts specifically for this purpose and use materials that they have created, quotes they have found, and data they have collected to get their message out into the global community. Imagine the power of asking students to use data collection to create infographics or satirical memes, or inviting them to use inspiration from their literature and their research to create videos—mini-documentaries or short-films—to post on social media or on a class website.

This project asks students to do all of the things they love: (1) vent about the problems that they face every day; (2) use Twitter in class; (3) post pictures, memes, quotes, and videos; (4) pull in friends and family to work with them; and (5) compete for likes and retweets. This is a fun and meaningful way to push their message and keep them engaged in their topics all throughout their research and authentic assessment in class.

ADDITIONAL RESOURCES

Teachers can consider incorporating all of these student-created writings into one larger piece:

1 All components of a research essay: letter of intent, annotated bibliography, essay, works cited page, notes page.
2 Nonfiction or fictional narrative.
3 Poetry (determine formatting based upon what you have or will be learning in class).
4 Resume and cover letter—have this discussion: Could what I'm researching lead to a potential career? If so, what does that look like?
5 Student-created visual—think memes, infographics, and pieces of artwork.
6 Campaign letter advocating for change to a person in position of power.
7 An accompanying digital video—think an advertisement, a public service announcement, or a documentary-style short film.

8 An interview with someone who has experienced the issue or who works in the field of interest.
9 Hours of community service/job shadowing in the field with an accompanying log and mentor evaluation.

CONCLUSION

Too often, teachers see their students consistently identifying problems without feeling like they have the power or autonomy to solve them. In a world that is shifting so quickly, it is essential that teachers arm students with the tools they need for positive change. This learning experience is a building block for authentic physical and digital engagement in students.

REFERENCES

Anderson, L. H. 2007. *Twisted*. New York: Viking.

Bower, D., B. Summers, R. Wilson, A. Sitaram, producers, and B. Summers, director. 2010. *Hungry for change* [Motion picture]. United Kingdom: SW Pictures Ltd.

Clarke, J. H. 2013. *Personalized Learning: Student-Designed Pathways to High School Graduation*. Thousand Oaks, CA: Corwin.

Crutcher, C. 2001. *Whale Talk*. New York: Greenwillow Books.

Giles, G. 2014. *Girls Like Us*. Somerville, MA: Candlewick Press.

Green, J. 2012. *The Fault in Our Stars*. New York: Dutton Books.

Hayn, J. A., J. S. Kaplan, and A. Nolen. 2011. "Young Adult Literature Research in the 21st Century." *Theory into Practice* 50 (3): 176–181. doi:10.1080/00405841.2011.584026.

Hopkins, E. 2004. *Crank*. New York: Simon Pulse.

Kittle, P. 2013. *Book Love: Developing Depth, Stamina, and Passion in Adolescent Readers*. Portsmouth, NH: Heinemann.

McDonald, J. 1997. *Swallowing Stones*. New York: Delacorte Press.

Mirra, N., D. Filipiak, and A. Garcia. 2015. "Revolutionizing Inquiry in Urban English Classrooms: Pursuing Voice and Justice through Youth Participatory Action Research." *English Journal* 2 (49): 49–57.

Romano, T. 1995. *Writing with Passion: Life Stories, Multiple Genres*. Portsmouth, NH: Boynton/Cook.

Rowell, R. 2013. *Eleanor & Park*. New York: St. Martin's Press.

Shakur, T. 1999. *The Rose That Grew from Concrete*. New York: MTV Books.

Thoreau, H. D. 1992. *Walden and resistance to civil government: authoritative texts, Thoreau's journal, reviews, and essays in criticism*. New York: Norton.

Part III

USING YOUNG ADULT LITERATURE AND DIGITAL SPACES TO ENGAGE IN THE WORLD

Chapter 6

Participating in Literacy and the Outside World: Consuming, Composing, and Sharing Graphic Narratives

Mike P. Cook and Brandon L. Sams

I like graphic novels. But, I would never teach them.

—Bethany, preservice teacher

Starting my year off with *American Born Chinese* was a great decision. My kids were challenged by the difficult topics. We formed a community. Reading it made so many other things possible.

—McKenzie, first-year teacher

In her work on literacy sponsorship, Brandt (1998) notes, "Sponsors are a tangible reminder that literacy learning throughout history has always required permission, sanction, assistance, [or] coercion" (167). Teachers and teacher educators are in a powerful position to shape what counts as reading and writing and what students believe to be possible through writing. For many years, teacher educators have been working under the specter of Lortie's (1975) "apprenticeship of observation"—how teachers have been taught in school is a powerful predictor of how they, themselves, will teach.

For preservice teachers (PSTs) who value and experienced traditional, monomodal literacy instruction in schools, a repetition of those same practices will simply not meet the twenty-first-century, multimodal literacy needs of grade six to twelfth students. The National Council of Teachers of English (2016), in the recently adopted statement *Professional Knowledge for the Teaching of Writing*, supports literacy instruction across a range of modes and technologies—multimodal composition—for various purposes and communication needs.

Teacher educators, who continue to support and sanction the traditional literacy practices and codex-canon centered textual identities and commitments of PSTs—to the exclusion of other literacy practices and pedagogies—will have done their present and future students a great injustice. Teacher educators, as literacy sponsors, are thus positioned to effect real change in terms of educating PSTs to adopt a robust sense of what counts as literacy in school.

It is vital for English Language Arts (ELA) teachers to prepare twenty-first-century literate and contributing citizens for a globalized world. As the nature of writing (and literacy) continues to evolve, students too must evolve and become effective composers of a variety of texts and text-types. One way for ELA and literacy educators to promote multimodal literacy development is through young adult literature (YAL), more specifically through reading graphic novels and composing graphic narratives. This work can begin in ELA methods classrooms with PSTs and then adjusted to address any sixth to twelfth classroom context.

USING GRAPHIC NARRATIVES TO RETHINK PRESERVICE TEACHER LITERACY INSTRUCTION

In order to foster twenty-first-century literacy development in students, teacher educators must rethink their work with PSTs by exploring new instructional approaches and providing their students opportunities to learn literacy skills and practices, including those focused on multimodal composition, particularly reading comics and graphic novels and composing graphic narratives. The term "graphic narrative" is used throughout this chapter, in place of "graphic novels and comics," because the texts used (e.g., read and composed) are narrative in nature—that is, they are stories, whether actual or fictional.

The instructional approach described next is useful for teachers with varied experience incorporating graphic narratives, in the classroom: those who already use graphic narratives (by providing new approaches, tools, and resources to augment their curricula) and those who are interested in incorporating graphic narratives but are unsure how (by providing multiple entry points to begin reading and composing graphic narratives with students). The unit includes rationales for instructional sequences and decisions, descriptions of reading and composing, and references to professional resources where readers can learn more.

In addition to its use in ELA methods courses (as discussed), the unit can be adapted and included in courses focused on YAL and methods courses focused on the teaching of reading, literature, and writing. The unit itself proceeds according to the following outline:

- Addressing Prior Experience and Creating Buy-In
- Consuming Graphic Narratives

- Composing Graphic Narratives
- Publishing Graphic Narratives
- Assessing Graphic Narratives

While it is important to note that consuming and composing (reading and writing) are reciprocal processes, and separating them is somewhat artificial, it has been done in the discussion of this unit in order to help the reader better follow the instructional approach, including the myriad mentor texts provided to students to support their reading and composing processes.

In order to provide additional clarity and context for the reader, it is necessary to make visible two instructional tenets guiding this curriculum, both of which connect to the philosophy of the National Writing Project.

The Classroom Is a Community of Practice

A community of practice is created through developing a shared disciplinary language; the use of disciplinary language by teachers and students guides goal setting, reading, composing, assessing, and sharing work.

Teachers of Writing Are Writers

When asking students to compose graphic narratives, and when composing their own, teachers must make their rhetorical and design thinking explicit and visible. As students struggle and triumph during the composing process, so do teachers, and the cojourney is a vital part of collective learning. Furthermore, learning to teach (multimodal) composing is not a spectator sport but occurs in the context of engaging in and intentionally reflecting on the skills, processes, and products of multimodal compositions. Educators learn to teach multimodal composition by composing multimodally.

WHY GRAPHIC TEXTS?

As a form of multimodal composition, graphic texts supports students' twenty-first-century literacy, including interacting with and making meaning from alphabetic and visual text and the combination. Analyzing and composing graphic texts addresses several standards (e.g., NCTE definition of twenty-first-century literacy, and Common Core State Standards). Students live in and communicate in a world in which content and modalities (visual and verbal) converge in increasingly complex ways. They must, therefore, be equipped to rhetorically navigate across modes and contexts, and composing multimodally leads to a more accurate and practical understanding of communication.

To help students develop the skills for multimodal composition, this unit incorporates YAL through graphic narratives into teacher education courses. These texts blend alphabetic text, images, and sounds, serving as a foundational genre for developing students' multimodal literacy skills. Graphic narratives are rhetorically complex, demanding that readers and composers consider word balloons, image and sequence, panel layout, color, and typography. In reading and composing graphic narratives, students make sense from and juxtapose two modalities (word and image) and make a variety of cognitively complex and rhetorical decisions.

Incorporating graphic texts into education courses fosters multimodal thinking, analysis, and literacy. The combination of text and image in graphic narratives requires active participation and creates meaning in unique and layered ways. As such, students must be able to effectively communicate and compose via multiple channels and through a variety (and combination) of modalities, which work together to create complex meaning. Responsible teaching, then, involves helping students understand that design and composing choices especially those that include visuals directly contribute to how their readers create meaning.

MULTIMODALITY, GRAPHIC NARRATIVES, AND PSTs

Part of the work of incorporating graphic narratives into teacher education should involve an examination of the types of texts we value in ELA classrooms, the ways in which we define literacy instruction, and our notions of preparing ELA teachers. First, it is important to expand the texts and literacy practices we sanction as school worthy to include multimodality. Second, we must acknowledge that graphic narratives serve as robust sites of multimodal literacy. And third, it is vital that we help PSTs to rethink and redefine their own perceptions of literacy instruction through the consumption and composition of multimodal texts such as graphic narratives.

Multimodality and Multimodal Literacy

Scholars argue for a rethinking and reconceptualization of literacy—and the often-used, traditional monomodal approach—to include all ways and forms of creating and sharing information (i.e., modes of communication). Literacy educators must move beyond traditional notions of literacy by adapting instruction to include a multitude of texts available via digital technology. To become fully literate, students need to communicate effectively in and across modalities; thus, responsible educators help students evolve as literate individuals who meet Yancey's (2004) and National Council of Teachers of English's (2011) call to become effective consumers and composers of multimodal texts.

Multimodal literacy requires readers to possess skills to not only negotiate a variety of layers and levels of meaning but make connections to both intra- and intertextual elements. Moreover, multimodal literacy asks students to understand how modes can be combined to create and compose meaning. It is no longer enough to make meaning through traditional literacy practices alone. It becomes increasingly important for literacy instruction to evolve accordingly. This call for an evolution within literacy instruction has served as a catalyst for the work with students described herein.

Graphic Narratives as Sites of Multimodal Literacy

Just as YAL can serve as powerful and relevant literacy sponsors, comics and graphic narratives are sophisticated sites of multimodality and effective sponsors of literacy and require readers to engage in a complicated and nuanced process of making meaning from multiple modes of communication, as well as the intersection of those modes. The graphic format, in fact, fosters deeper understanding and interpretation of literary elements, such as point of view, tone, and so forth, allowing readers to become active and comfortable consumers and analyzers of texts.

Reading graphic narratives can help students develop a range of transferrable literacy skills to decode, make connections to, and make meaning from an array of multimodal texts. Graphic texts can also foster critical thinking, assist students in developing new literacy skills, and improve students' multimodal literacy.

The process(es) of composing graphic narratives serve(s) as a bridge to other multimodal composing. Composition instruction must evolve with the times and embrace the concepts of creation and design and must value multimodal composing processes, like those seen in comics and graphic novels. In other words, composition instruction should address the need for an expanded view of and approach to multimodality, literacy, and meaning making. Comics offer students a robust experience analyzing and discussing the sophisticated rhetorical moves that composers utilize.

Likewise, they help students further deliberate their rhetorical considerations in their own compositions. While there are comparatively fewer voices calling for multimodal (and graphic narrative) composition in grades 6–12 literacy instruction, those who do point to a variety of benefits of graphic narratives, multimodal composition, and the intersection of the two. It is in this intersection, in an effort to help students become fully literate, that this graphic narrative instruction and multimodal work is grounded.

Preserve Teachers and Literacy Instruction

To ensure PSTs enter the classroom ready to employ multimodal literacy instruction with students, teacher educators must provide opportunities (1) to analyze multimodal and multimedia texts, (2) to develop a more comprehensive definition and understanding of literacy, and (3) to understand the multiple literacies that they and their future students use. Reading and literacy practices of PSTs determine their attitudes toward their own future literacy instruction.

Furthermore, the perceptions PSTs hold of the literacy practices they utilize in their own learning are important in determining how they will integrate multimodal literacy instruction into their own classrooms. As such, it is the responsibility of teacher educators to provide PSTs the space and time to explore their own perceptions of literacy practices and literacy instruction and to begin making connections to their future classrooms.

Graphic Narratives with PSTs

There is a dearth of information on the uses of graphic narratives with PSTs and their perceptions of literacy instruction; that said, there continue to be calls for a shift in teacher education programs to encourage PSTs to reconsider and redefine traditional literacy instruction, to experience and better understand the complexities accompanying literacy and literacy instruction, and to incorporate the world of YAL and multimodal texts into classrooms. For example, asking PSTs to focus their attention on multiple modalities and literacies aids in their awareness of the literacy practices their future students engage in.

Likewise, this practice can assist PSTs in designing instruction that fosters the development of multiple, powerful literacies. This includes the design of lessons based on images in graphic novels to encourage more critical questioning from students and the ability to make intertextual connections. If PSTs are to feel comfortable implementing multimodal literacy instruction in their classrooms, teacher educators must provide meaningful opportunities for them to learn from, explore, and design a range of text-types.

IMPLEMENTING GRAPHIC NARRATIVE CONSUMPTION AND CREATION IN THE CLASSROOM

Prior to implementing in the teacher education classroom, it is first important to assess PSTs' prior experiences with and perceptions of graphic narratives and to use this information to inform instruction. It is equally important to design intentional and guided opportunities for PSTs to interact with graphic narratives as consumers and then to use those experiences as they transition to composing their own graphic texts and ultimately to thinking about the literacy instruction they will provide students in their future classrooms.

Addressing Prior Experiences and Creating Buy-In

To help PSTs better understand the varied literacy practices students use inside and outside school, it is helpful to distribute reading and writing inventories. Invariably, students come to teacher education programs attached to and invested in traditional literacy practices. They consider themselves readers. And what counts as reading is, in the main, tied to the traditional textual body, the codex—and this attachment closely allied to American and British canons. These same students often report little familiarity with comics and graphic novels—or, at least, they are not willing to admit their experience.

Young teachers invest their identities in traditional, authoritative textual bodies as a cognitive and affective substitute for authority they lack. They are performing a teacher identity by investing in traditional literacies—ways of reading and writing that have, historically, been institutionally sanctioned and rewarded. Part of the job, then, as English teacher educators is to expand PSTs' understandings of what counts, in school and out, as legitimate literacy practices.

When students learn they will be reading and writing comics and graphic novels, they often share a few complaints: these are "boy books" and "these texts are too easy" among the most frequently announced. Few students have read graphic texts in school, making it difficult to sanction them as "real reading," echoing the long-held belief that graphic texts are read by younger and more inexperienced readers until they are ready for more ostensibly difficult, complex, "real" print text.

A side note: even after being convinced of the merit of graphic novels, students still hear resistance and condescension from area teachers. In order to convince students that reading and teaching graphic texts is a worthwhile enterprise that can promote critical and multimodal literacy development with students, educators can use a variety of different approaches, depending on situation and context.

If students have shown some comfort with ambiguity and confusion, it can be helpful to ask them to begin reading a graphic novel, such as *American Born Chinese*, without having first been prepped with background knowledge and support. This invites purposeful confusion and demands they attempt to solve interpretive problems on their own. This "deep-end" approach has the added advantage of approximating what their future students might experience when reading unfamiliar, complex texts. After immersing themselves in the graphic text, they are in a better position to understand and appreciate the support readings and instruction that come after.

For groups of students who are skeptical of the potential of graphic novels, in order to create buy-in, teacher educators can use several resources. Episodes 2 (2013) and 10 (2014) of the Literacy Research Association's *Research to Practice* series stress the value of graphic texts and teaching multimodal composition. The episodes feature researchers and teachers discussing the literacy practices of youth, sanctioned and unsanctioned literacy, and myriad ways young people use reading and writing to meet various communication needs.

Episode 2 focuses specifically on the reading of graphic novels in the classroom. This conversation among researchers and teachers helps students understand that what happens in school under the name of "reading and writing" can be so much more than reading canonical, print texts, and writing traditional essays—though these practices need not be lost.

Taken together, the episodes sanction a wide range of possibilities for literacy instruction—and students are especially persuaded by hearing from experienced teachers who have found success in teaching graphic novels. See the annotated resource section for other texts, websites, and podcasts that can be used to motivate and convince students of the value of multimodal literacy.

Consuming Graphic Narratives

Once students have begun rethinking and redefining literacy practices to include those that bridge the gaps between their own lives and their lived experiences in school, attention can be turned to effective multimodal literacy instruction. First, teacher educators can introduce PSTs to texts that help them understand how to read and make meaning from the graphic format.

There are a number of solid texts for this purpose, but three frequently used texts include Rudiger's (2006) article, "Reading Lessons: Graphic Novels 101," and select chapters from McCloud's (1993) *Understanding Comics, the Invisible Art,* and Frey and Fisher's (2008) *Teaching Visual Literacy: Using Comic Books, Graphic Novels, Anime, Cartoons, and More to Develop Comprehension and Thinking Skills.*

After this introduction, PSTs should receive guided opportunities to develop skills to interpret graphic narratives and to make them more comfortable with these text-types. Ultimately, students need to develop the skills and language of visual analysis, but because many students are new to graphic texts and to multimodal composition, it becomes important to provide support in a variety of ways. One way to provide such support is to provide and discuss with PSTs a glossary (see Box 6.1) of important format and visual terms (e.g., captions, panels, close-up, perspective, and coloring).

BOX 6.1.   EXCERPT OF COMIC GLOSSARY

Excerpt of Comic Glossary

Captions: Often placed in the top left-hand corner of a panel, this text provides exposition necessary to the understanding of the narrative

Panels: the individual frames that hold the content of the comic (e.g. image and text)

Close-up: A shot that focuses, extremely closely, on one element

Perspective: (1) One perspective can be looking up at an image, making it appear large (Ant's Eye); (2) another can be looking down on an image, making it appear small (Eagle Eye)

Coloring: This refers to the color of the image (the hue) and the intensity of the color (saturation)

Another useful support involves working with students to collaboratively analyze the conventions of graphic texts and to discuss devices such as tone, panel layout, establishing shot, contrast, and other design choices in multiple mentor texts (including mentor images and panels). (See Box 6.2 for sample collaborative analysis of a comic.)

BOX 6.2.   EXCERPT OF COLLABORATIVE ANALYSIS

Excerpt of Collaborative Analysis of *Detective Honeybear*

On the opening page, the class notes: variety of paneling and layout options used (creating specific perspective and tension); heavy use of black and white (creates a noir effect and established time); limited use of color (focus attention, visual foreshadowing)

As part of continued conversation, students discuss: author choice of panel layout (i.e., was this the best option?), the way in which tension was created (i.e., the early reveal of the main character), and so forth.

Beginning to think like composers, students use discussion and storyboarding to rethink and redesign the panel sequence on page one.

Detective Honeybear is a free comic available via Comixology.com

---

A third beneficial support for PSTs is to discuss how the artists' composing strategies and choices influence reading experiences and interpretations. This helps students to more deeply consider and better understand the rhetorical decisions and possibilities that they will negotiate during their own composing processes.

A key resource for mentor texts is Comixology (Iconology, 2016). This online, digital collection contains thousands of comics and graphic novels, many of them free and quality examples of effective multimodal design. Comixology also features a guided reading option, which focuses the reader's attention on the comic in a predetermined panel-by-panel, image-by-image, format. This is yet another scaffold for those new to the graphic format.

After reading and analyzing a variety of mentor texts, including those found on Comixology, such as *Detective Honeybear*, *The Superfogeys*, and *Archie*, along with traditionally published titles such as *Scott Pilgrim*, *American Born Chinese*, *Tomboy*, and others, students need opportunities to rethink and redesign select portions of artists' work. In their redesigns, they consider panel sequence, transition, proximity, and angle, among other concepts.

Students think about the ways writers and artists incorporate action and movement in their texts, which can lead to a more nuanced understanding of and skill in graphic composition. Students begin to understand what is essential to a panel, to a page, and to a narrative. During these conversations, PSTs can begin discussing the roles of mood, tone, and setting and their rationales for how they might use such devices in their own work. The goal is to prepare critical consumers and composers. The resources provided here are meant to offer a snapshot of potential resources to use with PSTs. For a more comprehensive bibliography, please consult the "Additional Resources for Educators—Learning More" section.

Composing Graphic Narratives

Once students have a foundational understanding of multimodal composition, they can apply those skills to their own. Students compose, publish, and share graphic texts in a variety of ways. Multiple tools and methods are available that account for the fluidity and diversity of processes involved in composing, publishing, and sharing information. Each of these tools—Microsoft Word and PPT, Comic Life, Prezi, and a variety of free online comic creation tools—offers users different affordances and constraints.

MS Word and PPT, for example, are programs students are already familiar with, allowing them to focus more on the composing process than on learning the tool. Comic Life, in contrast, provides a multitude of panels, images, and options for students, but using it requires more time to learn. Both options, however, provide students creative freedom throughout the composing process. Internet access is not required during composing. Students can upload their own images, select from a variety of filters, and easily publish their compositions on a variety of platforms.

Prezi is yet another possible composing tool. Similar to PowerPoint, Prezi allows users to make digital presentations; however, Prezi includes options for zooming and nonlinear reading. Much like the guided reading view in Comixology, students can choose to make some of the reading decisions for their audience by guiding their interaction with the graphic narrative, which requires rhetorical knowledge and savvy. Next is a model graphic narrative prompt (see Box 6.3) that readers can use or adapt in their own classrooms:

BOX 6.3.   GRAPHIC NARRATIVE PROMPT

For this assignment, you will utilize our in-class reading, viewing, and discussing graphic texts to drive your own composition. While you may choose your content, your composition should clearly draw from your interactions with and analysis of the comics we have read in class (e.g., on Comixology or the excerpted readings provided), those you have read on your own, and the scholarly texts we have discussed. In other words, you will use your reading and analysis of the ways in which these mentor authors have created and expressed their own ideas and rhetorical decisions. This assignment, ultimately, is for you to demonstrate your own understanding of visual rhetoric and literacy, ability to think critically, and ability to effectively compose using multiple modalities.

Publishing Graphic Narratives

Ultimately, a goal of teacher educators is to foster students' participation in their professional and digital worlds. To do this, students must go beyond simply composing graphic narratives by publishing and sharing their work with an extended digital audience. While there are myriad platforms for this, several stand out: blogs, YouTube, Twitter and social media, websites and ePortfolios, Amazon CreateSpace, and so on. These allow students to extend the influence beyond traditional classroom "publishing" methods to become active participants in the digital and literary worlds.

Moreover, digital publishing requires students to fully consider elements of design, visual rhetoric, aesthetics, and rhetorical situation, in order to communicate with others, to circulate their ideas, and to contribute to the field. The portion of the assignment prompt discussing publishing student work is available in Box 6.4.

BOX 6.4.   STUDENT PUBLISHING PROMPT

You may utilize any of the composing tools we have discussed in class (including hand drawing); remember to consider your rhetorical goals, along with the affordances (and potential constraints) of each tool as you make your decision. It is also important to remember that you will be publishing your graphic narrative digitally (using one of the methods we discussed in class—or perhaps your own idea); that is, it will be available for the world to see. Regardless of your approach, the final product should be professional and ready for a wide audience.

Finally, it is important to offer students the time to think metacognitively and to reflect on their experiences and learning. Requiring a reflection essay as part of the assignment can aid metacognitive thinking. Students are given specific prompts designed to guide their reflections and to value their voices and their descriptions of their composing processes. The final prompt component is provided in Box 6.5.

BOX 6.5.   STUDENT REFLECTION PROMPT

After completing your composition, you will also compose a reflection. This will be a hybrid essay, including images or panels from your graphic narrative as well as the mentor text(s) that informed your own. Your reflection should be a minimum of two double-spaced pages and should respond to three prompts. Please address/provide the following:

1 The composing and rhetorical decisions you made concerning images, text, color, paneling, and so on. Incorporate panels from your own graphic narrative and from your mentor text(s) and explain how these informed your composing process.
2 An explanation of your composing process (e.g., what tool did you utilize?), including a rationale for your choice.
3 A discussion of your digital publication method, why you chose to go this route, and how you feel it ultimately impacted (1) you as an author, (2) your composition as a whole, and (3) your audience.

Assessing Graphic Narratives

A major component of fostering understanding and practical skills development includes self- and peer-assessment. Students should be given ample opportunity to apply their knowledge in two ways: (1) as part of their composing and (2) in critical evaluation of not only their own products and process but also those of others at multiple stages of the composition process. While there are many considerations when it comes to assessing multimodal texts (e.g., content, organization, narrative, and process), utilizing a multimodal rubric can prove quite useful.

One option is adapted from Wyatt-Smith and Kimber's (2009) six concepts of multimodal assessment, including design, modal affordances, and cohesion, and Cook and Kirchoff's (2015) suggestion of a four-component design assessment (linguistic, visual, auditory, and overall design). The rubric itself comprises four Likert-style items—linguistic design, visual design, auditory design (this refers to the role of "sound" in the graphic format), and overall design—ranging from 1 (poor cohesion) to 5 (excellent cohesion).

For example, a rubric item might read: On the five-point scale provided (1 = poor cohesion to 5 = excellent cohesion), rate the composer's use of ____ in their design. Each student composer would receive a total score out of 20 points, which is easily converted to align with more traditional grading scales.

This approach empowers students and allows them to turn a critical eye to their and their peers' compositions and to simultaneously develop (1) a stronger and more nuanced understanding of multimodality and design; (2) a metalanguage for reading, discussing, and composing multimodal texts; and (3) a deeper understanding of their own composing and learning processes.

ADDITIONAL RESOURCES FOR EDUCATORS: LEARNING MORE

1　Sousanis, N. 2015. "Unflattening." *Podcast—New Books in Literary Studies*. https://podfanatic.com/podcast/new-books-in-literary-studies/episode/nick-sousanis-unflattening-5.

This podcast features an interview with Nick Sousanis, author of *Unflattening*, a book examining the philosophical roots of the privileging of text over image in contemporary thought and academic discourse. In this interview, Sousanis discusses his book, written as a graphic text, and the ways that exploring the relationship among image, text, visuals, and knowledge can transform schooling and education.

2　http://scholarlyvoices.org/unflattening/index.html.

This web resource is related to the reading and teaching of *Unflattening* and may be used by those wanting to explore creativity, multimodality, and visual thinking in relationship to reading and teaching graphic texts.

3 "Graphic Novels"—Episode 2, *Research to Practice* series. *Literacy Research Association.* https://www.youtube.com/watch?v=O95bOr_1bo0.

A conversation among scholars and teachers researching and teaching graphic novels, participants discuss latest research findings on graphic novels and literacy development and classroom applications. This resource might be used with PSTs at any stage of a unit or course of study on graphic novels or multimodal literacy instruction, to motivate study or to solidify classroom applications or research findings.

4 Yang, G. 2008. "Graphic Novels in the Classroom." *Language Arts* 85 (3): 185–92.

This short piece by Gene Yang, also the author of *American Born Chinese*, is composed in graphic format. While introducing the reader to the genre, he makes an argument for the inclusion of graphic texts in grades six to twelve classrooms.

5 Hansen, K. S. 2012. "In Defense of Graphic Novels." *English Journal* 102 (2): 57–63.

The author provides helpful resources for anyone looking to incorporate graphic novels in the classroom. She also anticipates common criticisms leveled at graphic novels and provides theoretically grounded responses teachers can use or adapt when defending their inclusion of graphic novels in the curriculum.

6 Schwarz, G. 2006. "Expanding Literacies through Graphic Novels." *English Journal* 95 (6): 58–64.

The author provides examples of how she scaffolds instruction to prepare students to read graphic novels. She includes examples of short comics, and how she uses them in her classroom, to support the development of critical, visual literacy skills that students transfer to longer graphic texts.

7 McCloud, S. 1993. *Understanding Comics.* New York: Harper Perennial.

In his seminal text, McCloud offers a user-friendly and in-depth introduction to the comic format. With chapters on reader participation, time, color, the creation process, and others, this serves as a useful introduction to reading and making meaning from comics and visuals in general.

8 Frey, N., and D. Fisher, eds. 2008. *Teaching Visual Literacy: Using Comic Books, Graphic Novels, Anime, Cartoons, and More to Develop Comprehension and Thinking Skills.* Thousand Oaks, CA: Corwin Press.

The authors offer readers a practical (i.e., grounded in the classroom) look at visual analysis and literacy as well as suggestions for using graphic novels and comics in classrooms. While portions of this text are outside the scope of approach described here, Chapters 1–3 often prove helpful in getting students discussing the role(s) of images and visual analysis in the ELA classroom.

9 Rudiger, H. M. 2006. "Reading Lessons: Graphic Novels 101." *Horn Book Magazine*, March/April: 128–134.

In this article, Rudiger guides readers, especially those new to the graphic format, through a detailed analysis of three comic pages. Here, the author walks readers through a scaffolded approach, beginning with vocabulary and increasing in complexity to panel layout and sequence, angle, and other ways of actively interacting with a graphic narrative. Furthermore, Rudiger's article serves as a starting point for those interested in incorporating graphic narratives into their own classrooms, as she walks readers through a panel-by-panel analysis.

10 Comixology (www.comixology.com).

Comixology is a digital comic and graphic novel platform offering readers tens of thousands of texts to choose from. While most include a purchase fee, there is also a rotating selection of free texts to choose from. Incidentally, the texts described in this unit for whole-class reading and analysis come from the list of free options. Additionally, Comixology is available online and through mobile apps, making it easily accessible for students. And as mentioned earlier, the platform offers a guided reading view that can be used to (1) introduce new readers to the graphic format and (2) analyze authorial decisions and their impact on readers and the reading process.

11 Graphic Novels and Comics as Mentor Texts

There is no shortage of texts that can serve as excellent mentors for students as they develop visual and multimodal analysis and composition skills. In fact, teachers should read widely and familiarize themselves with the options available before selecting the texts for use in their classrooms. That said, teachers and students engaged in this unit of instruction have experienced success using graphic novels such as *American Born Chinese, Scott Pilgrim, Tomboy, This One Summer, The Photographer, Pride of Baghdad, Daytripper, V for Vendetta*, and others, and online comics (see Comixology) such as *Detective Honeybear, The Superfogeys, Archie, Ms. Marvel, Secret Wars, The Authority*, and *Gotham Central*.

12 Composing Tools

Among the composing tools discussed and used with students in this unit are Microsoft Word and PowerPoint, Prezi, Comic Life, and a variety of online comic creation tools (e.g., Toondoo and Scholastic Graphix). It is also vital to allow students to create their compositions by hand if they feel (and can rationalize) that affords them the most rhetorical utility.

13 Publishing Platform

In this unit, students are encouraged to consider all publication options and to propose tools not considered or covered in class. However, it remains important to discuss a variety of options with them and offer them time to consider the relevant affordances and constraints to their individual compositions. Among those educators can discuss are blogs, websites and ePortfolios, Twitter and social media, YouTube, and Amazon CreateSpace (and other self-publishing outlets). While these are not meant to serve as a comprehensive list of available options or of what constitutes a "good" platform, they do provide students a glimpse into the myriad options and online spaces available to them, which promotes critical thinking, problem solving, and metacognition.

CONCLUSION

Engaging students in multimodal literacy practices helps them develop the skills necessary to be fully literate. This unit is designed to harness the power and relevance of YAL to engage teacher education students in the consumption and composition of graphic narratives. As part of this approach, educators can address students' prior experiences, create buy-in, and provide explicit guidance and support as students consume a variety of graphic narratives and compose their own.

To establish an authentic, real-world audience, students require opportunities to publish their graphic compositions in order to contribute to and share their voices with their disciplinary and digital worlds. Lastly, students benefit from meaningful and authentic opportunities to assess themselves and the work of their peers.

While this approach is discussed in the context of an ELA methods course for PSTs, the unit can be adjusted to fit a variety of courses and settings (e.g., YAL, 6–12 ELA classrooms). Likewise, the unit can be used by teachers with experience teaching graphic novels (those interested in new ideas) and those with little to no previous experience (those interested in incorporating graphic narratives into their classrooms but are unsure where to begin).

Readers should tweak this unit to fit their own needs, students, comfort levels, and so forth. Given the importance of helping students become multimodally literate and helping them create and share information through the interaction of multiple modes of communication (e.g., image and text), it is vital educators provide their students relevant and guided opportunities to practice, talk about, and develop the skills necessary to be fully literate in the digital and globalized world.

Teacher educators and teachers serve as powerful literacy sponsors and mentors through their curriculum choices and teaching approaches. This instructional unit is one way to alter what counts as literacy in school and how students become intentional readers and composers of a variety of texts. If, as has been suggested, teachers teach as they were taught, then the work of teacher educators serves as a mentor text for PSTs to expand their repertoire of instructional practices to account for the evolving twenty-first-century literacy needs of students.

REFERENCES

Brandt, D. 1998. "Sponsors of Literacy." *College Composition and Communication* 49 (2): 165–185.

Cook, M. P., and J. S. J. Kirchoff. 2015. "Graphic Novels in the Classroom: Suggestions for Appropriate Multimodal Writing Projects in Graphic Novel Units." *Minnesota English Journal.* https://minnesotaenglishjournalonline.org/.

Frey, N., and D. Fisher, eds. 2008. *Teaching Visual Literacy: Using Comic Books, Graphic Novels, Anime, Cartoons, and More to Develop Comprehension and Thinking Skills.* Thousand Oaks, CA: Corwin.

Iconology, Inc. 2016. "Comixology." https://www.comixology.com/.

Literacy Research Association. December 2, 2013. LRA Research to Practice Episode 2—Graphic Novels [video file]. https://www.youtube.com/watch?v=O95bOr_1bo0.

Literacy Research Association. August 10, 2014. LRA Show Episode 10 [video file]. https://www.youtube.com/watch?v=Ag4LUwyPRG4.

Lortie, D. C. 1975. *Schoolteacher: A Sociological Study.* Chicago: The University of Chicago Press.

McCloud, S. 1993. *Understanding Comics: The Invisible Art.* New York: Harper Perennial.

National Council of Teachers of English. 2011. *The NCTE Definition of 21st Century Literacies.* http://www2.ncte.org/statement/teaching-writing/.

National Council of Teachers of English. 2016. "Professional Knowledge for the Teaching of Writing." http://www.ncte.org/positions/statements/teaching-writing.

Rudiger, H. M. 2006. "Reading Lessons: Graphic Novels 101." *Horn Book Magazine,* March/April: 128–134.

Schwarz, G. 2006. "Expanding Literacies through Graphic Novels." *English Journal* 95 (6): 58–64.

Sousanis, N. June 12, 2015. "Unflattening." *Podcast: New Books in Literary Studies.* https://podfanatic.com/podcast/new-books-in-literary-studies/episode/nick-sousanis-unflattening-5.

Wyatt-Smith, C., and K. Kimber. 2009. "Working Multimodally: Challenges for Assessment." *English Teaching: Practice and Critique* 8 (3): 70–90.

Yancey, K. 2004. "Made Not Only in Words: Composition in a New Key." *College Composition and Communication* 56 (2): 297–328.

Yang, G. 2008. "Graphic Novels in the Classroom." *Language Arts* 85 (3): 185–192.

———. 2006. *American Born Chinese*. New York, NY: First Second.

Chapter 7

Remixing Literacy for Justice and Hope

Breanne Huston

When we accept that true love is rooted in recognition and acceptance, that love combines acknowledgment, care, responsibility, commitment, and knowledge, we understand there can be no love without justice.

—bell hooks (2014, 103–104)

"Same old same old" is as familiar to the rhetoric that surrounds education in the United States as whiteboards and rows of desks. The following excerpts from recent essays written by high school students in the Southeast convey the sentiments of many students across the nation:

When I am asked to describe a traditional classroom, I picture white walls and dusty books. I see students in the latest Aéropostale jeans blankly staring at the clock as they count down the minutes until lunch. There is no challenge. There is no enjoyment. There are only empty vessels who are expected to be filled by knowledge.

—Ess (pseudonym, 17)

School has taught me a lot more about how screwed up the world is than it has taught me over the curriculum information we're supposed to learn. It has made me realize you can't trust someone no matter what their level of authority is. School is almost like a prison because they tell you when not to talk, when to eat, when not to eat, and when to go to the bathroom and when not to go. Unfortunately, this is the world we live in and people will just have to accept it.

—Jay (pseudonym, 16)

Sound familiar? As standardization and accountability in schools kick into overdrive, many teachers and students feel the loss of power. In a place where boundaries, benchmarks, and boxes are becoming the norm, it may seem that the only option is to give in to the demands of the system. For educators feeling this pressure and wanting to resist it for themselves and for their students, there is another option, one that teachers all over are choosing: the remixing of education toward a more just vision of school.

Columbia University Professor Lalitha Vasudevan explains that this remixing, or reimagining, of education occurs through the "reconfiguration of texts, technologies, and resources . . . by the same youth who are often marginalized in school contexts" (2010, 64). The combination of young adult novels and new technologies opens up a number of spaces for teachers and students to explore and remix together. Critical literacy, which aims to move past monologic understandings privileged in schools across the country, is an important theoretical underpinning of this work.

CRITICAL LITERACY

The works of Jones (2006), Vasudevan (2010), and hooks (1994) provide entryways for creating powerful spaces for students and educators. In her book *Teaching to Transgress*, bell hooks describes transgressive teaching as "a movement against and beyond boundaries" and education as "the practice of freedom" (1994, 12). With roots in poststructuralism and critical theory, a critical literacy approach to education positions schools as spaces where students and teachers transcend imposed barriers, disrupt assumptions, examine relations of power, and learn to question and act.

Jones (2006) compares critical literacy to "a pair of eyeglasses that allows one to see beyond the familiar and comfortable" (67). The practice of challenging assumptions and the status quo is important not only for the critical thinking skills that schools commonly value but also for mindfully bringing the lived experiences of students into literacy activities. How educators go about this work will vary because students' lives vary.

Jones and Hughes (2016) remind us that there are "infinitely different ways that bodies/places/discourses/materiality come together to produce relations of power" (178). This idea is both daunting and exciting. It may be an overwhelming experience for a teacher to contemplate all of the factors that are colliding in the classroom at once, but these infinite collisions also invite infinite critical practices. In other words, the acceptance that there is not just one "right" way to practice critical literacy invites experimentation, play, dialogue, and openness.

Jones tells us that "a critical literacy lens focuses on three interrelated *layers*: perspective, positioning, and power; and engages in three foundational *tenets:* deconstruction, reconstruction, and social action" (2006, 67). Thinking about these layers and tenets, defined in Box 7.1, and how they may be foregrounded in literacy activities will help teachers be more critical in their practices.

**BOX 7.1.   LAYERS AND TENETS OF CRITICAL
LITERACY AS DEFINED BY JONES (2006, 75–85)**

Three Layers of Critical Literacy

> *Perspective:* refers to the creator of the text, the text itself, and the
> reader
> *Positioning:* the placement of someone or something by someone or
> something through language and/or ideology
> *Power:* is always moving and shifting and is used depending on the
> context in which people are relating and the people themselves

Three Tenets of Critical Literacy

> *Deconstruction:* to take apart texts, identities, systems, and structures
> bit-by-bit to unveil power, perspective, and positioning
> *Reconstruction:* the recreation and reconfiguration of texts, identi-
> ties, systems, and structures so that new iterations of power, per-
> spective, and positioning may be represented and foregrounded
> *Social action:* working toward change in all shapes and sizes

---

The four activities described in this chapter infuse technology with Sherman Alexie's young adult novel *The Absolutely True Diary of a Part-Time
Indian* (2007). The activities encourage students to make (dis)connections to
their own lives and to the world as they read, write, think, question, and act.
Threaded throughout is the goal of remixing the standard literacy curriculum
by disrupting binary structures encountered by students in their lives. Educators
are invited to engage in critical literacy and transgressive teaching by remixing
these activities, described briefly in Box 7.2, for and with their own students.

BOX 7.2.   SUMMARY OF ACTIVITIES

Activity 1: Kittens, Puppies, and Podcasts

> Students use the choice of kittens or puppies to understand binary
> oppositions and to think about the role of categories and of
> the meaning often assigned to them. The activity integrates an

Invisibilia podcast called "The Power of Categories" to help students understand the broader implications of binary thinking.

Activity 2: Photographing Binaries in School Space

After discussing binaries imposed upon the protagonist of *The Absolutely True Diary of a Part-Time Indian,* students use cameras to create visual representations of binaries at work in their own school space. They produce written deconstructions of their binaries and upload both to the class website.

Activity 3: There, I Fixed It

Students channel the spirit of a social media meme to reconstruct the binaries photographed in activity 2.

Activity 4: Entering the Dialogue

Students select a social issue and create their own text as they themselves enter the dialogue.

Remixing *The Absolutely True Diary of a Part-Time Indian* and Binary Oppositions

The Absolutely True Diary of a Part-Time Indian (2007) is an accessible text for students to anchor their critical work and to apply Jones's layers and tenets. The narrator, Junior, is a high school freshman with (dis)abilities who leaves his reservation in Spokane to attend an all-white high school thirty miles away. The alienation felt by Junior is perhaps most clear when he dryly remarks that the only other Indian in his new school is the mascot. Through Junior and his story, Alexie uses humor to address critical issues of not only race but also class, gender, education, abuse, alcoholism, and even death.

Junior narrates his experience in a lot of what are called binaries. The concept of binaries is a helpful starting place in a critical literacy approach. Binaries are pairs of related terms that are treated as essential opposites and are indicative of power and privilege. Major identity binaries include male/female, wealthy/poor, able/disabled, and white/nonwhite. In these oppositions, the first term is dominant and privileged over the second.

All of these binaries contribute to the master binary self/other. Binaries in Junior's life include identity oppositions such as wealthy/poor, white/nonwhite, and able/disabled and others that are important to his position as a fourteen-year-old boy in school such as teacher/student, popular/unpopular, and smart/dumb.

The impetus for Junior's decision to leave the school on his reservation occurs on his first day of high school when he looks in his math book and sees his mother's name written inside the front cover. You see, Junior loves math. A lot. He has been looking forward to elevating his learning experiences in high school, especially through math class, and when he sees that he has been issued the same math book that his mother had decades earlier, the shabby state of the resources in his school overwhelms him. Angry at the inequity, he flings the book across the room and hits his math teacher, Mr. P., in the face, breaking his nose. Junior is suspended.

Junior's feelings about his school are not so different from those expressed by Ess and Jay in the introduction. Ess writes of "white walls and dusty books," while Jay writes about "how screwed up the world is." These three examples all occurred in the last decade; yet, they are products of an institution that has been at work for 300 years—school. Jones's three Ps (power, perspective, and positioning) and three tenets of critical literacy (deconstruction, reconstruction, and social action) will help teachers and students think about not only how structures and systems came to be and who they benefit but also how they can be remixed.

One of the ultimate goals of critical literacy is that students create a space where they are working together for social change. This means that they must learn to trust one another. A safe place for individual exploration is important, but if students stay there, they may not see that change is possible—or worse, they may not see that it is needed. If students do not have personal connections to the literature, binary thinking and marginalization may seem either like someone else's problem or something that just makes for a good story. Even students who do have many connections to the literature may feel overwhelmed by the obstacles.

It is important to search for common ground, for a way that students can begin to think and act together. It is also important to help students deconstruct the human need or tendency to categorize that is at the heart of binary oppositions so that they can understand why this practice persists. The introductory activity described next, called "Kittens, Puppies, and Podcasts," is designed to do that through the imposition of an essential question: kittens or puppies?

Activity 1: Kittens, Puppies, and Podcasts

Often (over)used in elementary schools as a persuasive writing prompt, the choice between kittens or puppies may help secondary students understand the concept of binaries and how they can be problematic at best. The goal of this activity is for students to be mindful about the function of categories in everyday life. Categories may help us to function and create order, but they may also define people in terms that are too strict, limiting the possibilities that are available to individuals. The binary choice between the popular pets serves as a metaphor for identity categories that many are not empowered to choose. Box 7.3 will help focus this activity.

BOX 7.3. QUESTIONS TO USE WITH "KITTENS, PUPPIES, AND PODCASTS"

- Why do we categorize?
- Is this tendency innate?
- Are the categories themselves natural, or do we create them, or is it some of both?
- When does categorizing become problematic?

When teachers first pose this question (kittens or puppies?) to students, it is important to "force" them to select from the options available to them, of which there are only two: kittens or puppies. They may not choose "both," and they may not choose "neither." It is likely that some students will enthusiastically select kittens, others will enthusiastically select puppies, and still others will struggle with the decision.

It is helpful to have students write a brief description or explanation of their choice and then use their writing to guide them into a class discussion. Teachers may begin by asking for a show of hands to determine who picked kittens and who picked puppies. A few student volunteers may be asked to use their writing to express why or how they made their choice.

After students share, teachers should pose a different question: how difficult was it to make this choice, and why? This question will begin to disrupt the imposition of the binary choice by allowing students who struggled with it to explain why. Some students may take the opportunity to express their love for both kittens and puppies, while others may explain that they simply do not care for either. Still others may voice a preference for bunnies, snakes, fish, or hamsters.

Teachers can use students' responses to facilitate a discussion about categories, false binaries, and relations of power that are always part of such structures. For example, in addition to considering the fixed nature of categories, students may find it helpful to discuss the characteristics that are usually assigned to dog people (e.g., fun-loving, energetic, and friendly) and those usually assigned to cat people (e.g., loner, quiet, and shy) and then think about the extent to which those descriptions are true for them and why they exist in the first place.

To break down classroom walls and illustrate an application of the choices, teachers may integrate a seven-minute clip from the February 5, 2015, episode of NPR's *Invisibilia*, "The Power of Categories." The hosts talk about the tip-generating strategy of RISE Coffee Shop in New York, which draws on the human tendency to categorize. Each day, RISE baristas place two different tip jars on the counter with a binary question posed to their patrons. Whichever tip jar ends up with the most money indicates the "winner." This competition has increased tips dramatically. The choice highlighted in this *Invisibilia* segment is, helpfully, kittens or puppies.

The podcast hosts transition from the description of RISE's tip strategy to an experiment involving babies' reactions to seeing pictures of cats and dogs. According to the researcher featured in the segment, babies react to pictures of cats and dogs differently, suggesting an innate ability to categorize. In this seven-minute audio clip, students are exposed to engaging and digestible commentary on pop culture and scientific research connected to the work they are doing in class with binaries and literature.

This introductory activity creates shared experiences for students and teachers about binaries that can then be used to move into an area that is a little more personal for students and that deals more explicitly with questions of power, perspective, and positioning. The follow-up activity discussed next, "Photographing Binaries in School Space," uses the momentum from "Kittens, Puppies, and Podcasts" and students' (dis)connections with *The Absolutely True Diary of a Part-Time Indian* to invite students to think critically about a space in which they spend a lot of their time: school.

Activity 2: Photographing Binaries in School Space

The goals of this activity are for students to (1) broaden their interpretation of binary oppositions; (2) recognize that regardless of the privileges their identity categories afford them personally, binary structures affect everyone who is a member of a community; and (3) learn that differences and similarities exist among classmates at the same time.

This activity, which has students taking photographs of their school space and then deconstructing them, works well in connection with *The Absolutely True Diary of a Part-Time Indian* because many of the book's conflicts take place in and around issues and situations related to school. Students begin by identifying and discussing the binaries imposed upon Junior by his school. The excerpt in Box 7.4 illustrates the interplay between schools and binary categories in *The Absolutely True Diary of a Part-Time Indian*.

In the illustrative passage, Mr. P. is encouraging Junior to leave the reservation school for the neighboring public school by describing the oppressive conditions that have existed there. Immediately evident in the passage is the binary white/Indian. Students will also likely have little trouble identifying teacher/student and even acceptable/unacceptable behavior.

BOX 7.4.   EXCERPT FROM *THE ABSOLUTELY TRUE DIARY OF A PART-TIME INDIAN*

"When I first started teaching here, that's what we did to the rowdy ones, you know? We beat them. That's how we were taught to teach you. We were supposed to kill the Indian to save the child."

"You *killed* Indians?"

"No, no, it's just a saying. I didn't literally kill Indians. We were supposed to make you give up being Indian. Your songs and stories and language and dancing. Everything. We weren't trying to kill Indian people. We were trying to kill Indian culture." (Alexie, 2007, 35)

To help students identify additional binary oppositions in the novel and in their own schools, teachers may find it helpful to pair the passage in Box 7.4 with the one in Box 7.5, from the work of critical media educational researchers Alvermann and Hagood (2000). This passage helps foreground other binary oppositions as they think about the novel and their own school. Students will need help with words such as "discourse" and "pedagogical," but will likely have no trouble distinguishing the binaries: inclusion/exclusion, work/pleasure, acceptable/unacceptable, teacher/student, classroom/playground, mind/body, and in-school/out-of-school literacies.

BOX 7.5.   EXCERPT FROM ALVERMANN AND HAGOOD (2000)

Over the last 300 years, American schooling has become a particular discourse. A separate and distinct entity from other discourses, the discourse of school forms spaces of inclusion and exclusion, from which dichotomies are etched into acceptable or unacceptable practices. School design, pedagogical implementation, and relations between teachers and students highlight distinctions between work and pleasure, classroom and playground, in-school and out-of-school literacies, teacher and student, and mind and body within school discourse. Those aspects have influenced the ways in which the discourse of school establishes itself as an institution with various, yet separate, spaces for thought and pleasure. (2000, 199)

Just as the experiment discussed in the *Invisibilia* podcast helps students to see real-world applications of binaries, the appearance of this passage in a scholarly journal will give students the academic permission to productively critique schools through their own work. The goal of this pairing is not to suggest to students that schools are evil places only causing harm; rather, it invites them to think about the ways in which the system works. The questions in Box 7.6 may guide this work.

**BOX 7.6.   QUESTIONS TO GUIDE
"PHOTOGRAPHING BINARIES IN SCHOOL"**

- What conditions make it possible for binaries to exist in schools?
- When do people (or you) benefit? Who benefits? When do people (or you) suffer? Who suffers?
- How could school exist differently?

After students have examined binaries in *The Absolutely True Diary of a Part-Time Indian* and their effects on Junior, his peers, and his family, they will be ready to notice and deconstruct binaries in their own school space. Working in small groups, students may use their cell phones or other digital cameras made available to them to snap pictures of binaries represented in their school.

The possibilities for binaries abound. Some common examples include photographs of the boys' bathroom next to the girls' to represent male/female, a large teacher's desk next to a smaller student desk to illustrate teacher/student, a classroom juxtaposed to the cafeteria to show work/play, the school's trophy case filled with sports memorabilia next to the theater stage for sports/arts, and an assignment alongside a failing one to demonstrate right/wrong. Figures 7.1 to 7.5 display the work of some students who participated in this activity at Ess and Jay's school.

After students take their binary photographs, they may upload them along with a written deconstruction to the class website. The questions in Box 7.7 will help students with the deconstruction and reimagining of their visual binary.

Figure 7.1.   United States/world visual binary.

**BOX 7.7.   QUESTIONS TO HELP STUDENTS
DECONSTRUCT THEIR VISUAL
BINARY IN ACTIVITY 2**

- Who usually benefits from this binary?
- Why do they benefit? How is the "other side" affected? In what situations might the other side benefit?
- Why is it this way?
- How did it come to be?
- How could it be another way?
- Who does not fit?

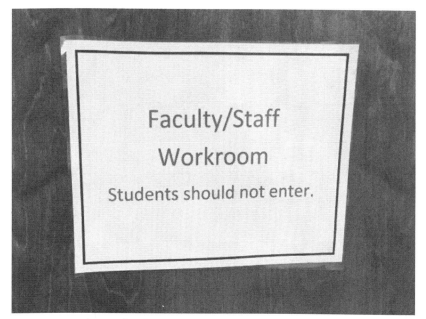

Figure 7.2. Teacher/student binary.

Figure 7.3. Wealthy/poor binary.

Figure 7.4. Male/female binary.

This activity allows students to use a medium that they are comfortable with (e.g., the cameras on their phones or ones that are provided to them) to critically connect their own school space with the literature they are studying and to begin to discuss how power operates and positions people in the world. Through their photography and writings, students have identified, deconstructed, and begun the work of reconstructing binary oppositions. The final two activities discussed in this chapter build upon this work to engage students in the further reconstruction, repositioning, and remixing of binaries and to move students toward social action.

Activity 3: There, I Fixed It

In a 2017 Red Clay Writing Project institute, writer, researcher, and educator Dr. Stephanie Jones shared a social media meme called "There, I Fixed It" with K–12 educators in Georgia and encouraged them to imagine ways they could integrate the meme into their students' learning. This meme has cropped up on social media sites like Instagram and Twitter and shows users "fixing" the posts of other users that they find troubling.

After sharing their visual binaries from the previous activity, students may work to reconfigure or reconstruct them into more just positions. Using

Figure 7.5. Truth/fiction binary.

available software like Photoshop, or any number of free apps on their phones, students edit their photographs and those of their classmates. Photographs may also be printed out to edit by hand. Each new creation should be captioned with the phrase "There, I Fixed It." This activity will not only help students remix binary structures present in their schools but also help them reimagine their positions as active, thinking, critical members of a community whose beliefs and actions matter.

Activity 4: Entering the Dialogue for Justice

When students have worked through several structured activities designed to help them think critically about binaries and issues of justice, they will be ready for a larger literacy project. In this culminating activity, students are encouraged to select a social issue that they care about, want to learn more about, and feel moved to act upon. Ultimately, students will create a text to share with an authentic audience (in other words, any one or number of people other than just their teacher) that raises awareness of the perspectives, positions, and relations of power implicated by and through their chosen issue.

The students should be encouraged to think about the message they want to communicate and the genre that will help them to do that effectively. Possible texts include (but certainly are not limited to) blogs, TED Talks, podcasts, spoken word, essays, art galleries, and poems.

Teachers may provide a central publishing location for students' work, such as the school website, but they can think of ways to help students share their work with larger audiences. For example, students may create a gallery of their work in the school's media center and invite other classes to visit it. They may also organize a coffee shop gathering and consider inviting community members. Teachers might also think cross-curricularly and reach out to journalism, video broadcasting, yearbook, art, and literary magazine teachers and sponsors about working on a project together.

Through their study of binaries, schools, and *The Absolutely True Diary of a Part-Time Indian*, students have worked with and across issues of class, race, education, and ability, but the issues chosen by students may or may not relate directly to the novel. Teachers will need to supplement this activity with outside resources such as news and magazine articles, blog posts, and media clips to broaden students' understanding of the issues they wish to study.

Real-world examples show students the different ways their voices can be heard. Box 7.8 contains a list of possible texts and sites that can be used to not only expand the knowledge of students but to help them imagine ways to enter the dialogue themselves. The nature of the mini lessons and the amount of structure provided will depend on the students and the topics that they

**BOX 7.8. ADDITIONAL RESOURCES TO USE
AS STUDENTS ENTER THE DIALOGUE**

TED Talks

- "The Danger of a Single Story" by Chimamanda Ngozi Adichie

  https://www.ted.com/talks/chimamanda_adichie_the_danger_of_
  a_single_story

- "We Should All Be Feminists" by Chimamanda Ngozi Adichie

  https://www.youtube.com/watch?v=hg3umXU_qWc

- "We Need to Talk about an Injustice" by Bryan Stevenson

  https://www.ted.com/talks/bryan_stevenson_we_need_to_talk_about_
  an_injustice

Brave New Voices

- "Feminism" by Denver Team, 2014

  https://www.youtube.com/watch?v=4fiOSGvYMBA

- "Why Are Muslims So . . .?" by Detroit Team, 2015

  https://www.youtube.com/watch?v=3_i7wELTVi0&t=77s

- "Emmett" by Philadelphia Team, 2015

  https://www.youtube.com/watch?v=RrizMMiBbBY

Documentaries and TV Episodes

- MTV's *Rebel Music: Native America: 7th Generation Rises*

  https://www.youtube.com/watch?v=-aRwprNai4A

- Miss Representation

  https://www.youtube.com/watch?v=FZYpAuUzDhU

- The Mask You Live In

  Netflix and http://therepresentationproject.org

- *Class Divide*

  www.hbo.com

Websites

- The Representation Project

  http://therepresentationproject.org/

- The Equal Justice Initiative

  http://eji.org/

- This I Believe

  http://thisibelieve.org/

choose. The important part is that students feel empowered to use their work to take a stand.

CONCLUSION: TOWARD JUSTICE AND HOPE

It is difficult to call the end of Junior's story a happy one. While he does find inner strength as he overcomes obstacles, learns that people are more complex than they may initially seem, and makes amends with his child-hood best friend, Junior also loses some of the people closest to him through tragedies with alcohol, discovers that his new school has its own set of problems, and realizes that his closest friend's future is uncertain at best. Indeed, he is both a little better *and* a little worse. He is, in a word, changed.

It is in this way, too, that Junior is much like the students who fill classrooms everywhere. They will all leave their schools different from how they arrived, and the paths they will take are innumerable. Ess left her school for an Ivy League university; Jay left without a high school diploma.

All students will leave changed. The experiences afforded them while they are part of our schools will be part of them forever, and they will affect their communities and the world in ways that are both clear and untold. This cycle can be creative and healing. When educators choose to transgress against barriers, to help students reimagine and remix what schools can be, and to challenge assumptions and entrenched relations of power, they are choosing to work toward a more just classroom and a more hopeful world for everyone.

REFERENCES

Alexie, S. 2007. *The Absolutely True Story of a Part-Time Indian*. New York: Hachette Book Group.

Alvermann, D., and M. Hagood. 2000. "Critical Media Literacy: Research, Theory, and Practice in 'New Times'." *Journal of Educational Research* 93 (3): 193–205.

hooks, b. 1994. *Teaching to Transgress: Education as the Practice of Freedom*. New York: Routledge.

———. 2014. *Feminism is for Everybody: Passionate Politics* [Kindle PC version]. Retrieved from Amazon.com.

Jones, S. 2006. *Girls, Social Class, and Literacy: What Teachers Can Do to Make a Difference*. Portsmouth, NH: Heinemann.

Jones, S., and H. Hughes. 2016. "Changing the Place of Teacher Education: Feminism, Fear, and Pedagogical Paradoxes." *Harvard Educational Review* 86 (2): 116–182.

Miller, A., and L. Spiegel. February 6, 2015. "The Power of Categories." *Invisibilia Podcast*. http://www.npr.org/programs/invisibilia/384065938/the-power-of-categories.

Vasudevan, L. 2010. "Education Remix: New Media, Literacies, and the Emerging Digital Geographies." *Digital Culture & Education* 2 (1): 62–82.

Chapter 8

#iread #iwrite #iteach: Mashing Up Participatory Culture and Critical Inquiry with YAL in the ELA Classroom

Steffany Comfort Maher

> Power is everywhere; not because it embraces everything but because it comes from everywhere.
>
> —Michel Foucault (1990)

The idea of creating remixes and mashups in the English Language Arts (ELA) classroom is exciting—having fun assignments where students will engage in reading, writing, and creating by bringing into the classroom technology they are familiar with from their engagements outside the classroom is precisely what English teachers dream of and what scholars in English education are calling for (Elliot-Johns, 2012). However, English teachers also want their students to question and read analytically, to explore complicated ideas and materials, to foster their imagination, and to become critically thinking citizens in a culturally diverse and still-developing democracy.

So how do teachers help their students to think, read, and respond critically while also engaging with texts and one another? A critical inquiry approach to teaching young adult literature (YAL) enables teachers to foster student engagement and critical thinking and reading skills, while effectively incorporating technology into the classroom helps students engage with assignments, one another, and the wider world.

Combining critical inquiry with the examination and creation of remixes and mashups is an opportunity for students to connect popular culture with critical pedagogy. A critical inquiry approach to teaching asks critical questions about issues in the lives of students and in the world; and drawing on material read in class, such as M. T. Anderson's *Feed* (2002) and Rainbow Rowell's *Eleanor & Park* (2013), creating remixes and mashups in response to those questions could bring about exciting results.

THEORETICAL FRAMEWORK: A CRITICAL
INQUIRY APPROACH

A critical inquiry approach to teaching YAL not only brings an important critical aspect to the study of these texts but also provides a means of student engagement with the texts, one another, and the wider world. Critical inquiry is derived from critical theory and critical pedagogy approaches, as well as pragmatic philosophies of inquiry. The aim of social critical theory is to recognize the systems of power within a society as well as to learn the means to change these systems so groups of people are no longer marginalized or oppressed within that society (Horkheimer, 1982).

A critical pedagogy approach connects critical theory and education. This philosophy invites teachers and students to learn together in what Paulo Freire (2000) calls a "problem-posing method" of teaching, in which the teacher and students consider materials in class, share their own positions on them, and reconsider their positions as others share their own ideas. A critical pedagogy approach focuses on raising consciousness of power struggles within a society and how knowledge affects and is affected by those structures.

Examining popular culture is an excellent way to raise awareness of power structures within society. Connections between YAL and popular culture are easily made. Students may be able to grasp these connections quickly, yet inquiring into the messages they relate may take a bit more effort. And thinking critically about how to respond to those messages requires more effort still.

The final component of critical inquiry is inquiry. Inquiry is derived from philosophies of logic, and Charles Sanders Peirce contends that in inquiry, three components work together to form conclusions or beliefs: abduction, deduction, and induction (Santaella, 1997). Thus, critical inquiry is a bringing together of critical theory, critical pedagogy, and inquiry. In the classroom, critical inquiry allows students to ask their own questions related to their rising consciousness (Giroux, 2010).

In a classroom devoted to critical inquiry, students and teacher learn from one another. By critically reading, responding, discussing, writing, presenting, and teaching together, both analyze texts for critical, historical, and cultural understanding. Writing, then, becomes a mode for critical inquiry into a variety of subjects, including the social and historical dimensions of genre and grammar. As students work through this process of critical inquiry and use technology they may already know, they respond critically to what they are reading and learning in powerful ways. One genre with which students are most likely familiar is the meme.

ANALYZING POP CULTURE: MEME ADVERTISEMENTS
AND SUBVERTISEMENTS

One need only open up their social media feed to see how powerful the meme is. Memes are everywhere. Connecting YAL with memes and other visual literacies is a powerful means to engage students in the classroom and to get them thinking critically about what they are reading. For example, Steffany asked students in her introduction to literature course (a course she designed to focus on YAL) to read Anderson's *Feed*. This YA novel is set in the future, when the Internet—the "Feed"—is implanted directly into the brain in childhood.

All those who can afford the Feed can chat directly with one another through it, watch any television program or film they choose, and purchase and ship items directly to themselves whenever they want, as advertisements appear directly in their Feed. When Titus and his friends' Feeds are hacked on a trip to the moon, Titus meets Violet, who has also been hacked, and she helps him to think critically about his Feed for the first time. This novel is a strong critique of the dominance of corporate advertising and of media-dominated culture.

While teaching this text, Steffany incorporated meme advertisements from large corporations, and she and her students discussed the messages these advertisements were promoting. A "meme" can be defined in several different ways, but the definition Steffany used with her students was from the online Merriam-Webster (2017) dictionary: "an amusing or interesting item (such as a captioned picture or video) or genre of items that is spread widely online especially through social media."

Students examined clothing and technology advertisements because these advertisements are often targeted to teenage audiences, and similar advertisements often pop up in feed. A quick Google search provided her class with images of Apple product advertisements showing close-ups of the Apple product, often with just a hand holding the item or a finger pointing toward it.

Recent Calvin Klein advertisements portray a model, singer, or actor wearing some type of Calvin Klein undergarment and the slogan "I ____ in #mycalvins": "I seduce in #mycalvins;" "I make money in #mycalvins;" "I excel in #mycalvins."

In class, students read these advertisements, and in small groups, they discussed the messages the advertisements portray. The groups then shared their analyses with the class, and Steffany facilitated a large-group discussion on the underlying ideologies in the advertisements.

Afterward, students moved back into small groups and applied Rob Pope's concept of "textual intervention" in order to think and respond

Figure 8.1.   An Apple advertisement for iPad 2.

critically to these texts. "Playing" with text is not a deviation from critical inquiry—it is an essential component. Playing with a text provides new ways of considering the text; it enables the critical reader to look at it from different perspectives.

Pope (1995) argues that the best way to understand a text and how it "works" is "to change it: to play around with it, to intervene in it in some way (large or small), and then to try to account for the exact effect of what you have done" (1). One example of textual intervention is "subvertising." Subvertising is a form of culture jamming that subverts media culture and critiques mainstream corporate advertising. Combining subvertising with a YA novel like *Feed* can get students thinking critically about advertisements.

Once students had the opportunity to critique *Feed* and the advertisements in class, through reading, discussing, and writing, Steffany shared some examples of subvertisements with her students. One subvertisement appropriate to teach with *Feed* is a mashup meme created by Adbusters (www. adbusters.org) in which a seemingly white adult hand is holding an iPad out so that the reader can see the long edge of it, how thin it is.

This is similar to the first Apple advertisement Steffany had shown her students, and to many Apple advertisements touting the thinness of their products. The text reads, "Thinner than ever." And on the other side of the iPad is an image of a starving black child naked from the waist up, reaching out toward the iPad. There is evidence of malnutrition in his thin body—clearly showing his ribs—and in his thin arm, hair, and face.

Rich discussion was born from this and other memes aimed at subverting mainstream media and advertising. Students quickly noted the use of irony in subvertising, and they were eager to try it out themselves.

Figure 8.2. Two Calvin Klein advertisements.

Once Steffany and her students had an opportunity to analyze and discuss these memes, the students created their own mashups, taking popular advertisements and "intervening." Pope recommends that students play with the texts in small groups first, aiming at creating two interventions: "one subtle; the other outrageous" (4). Students worked on this in their small groups during class. They then discussed why they made the interventions they did, as Steffany asked what "preferences" the change(s) implied or asserted (5).

After "playing around" with these texts in groups during class, students chose their own advertisements, analyzed them individually, and subverted them by addressing issues important to them. They used meme generators, such as http://www.memes.com/generator, created their own subvertisements, and posted them on their class blogs. Finally, students presented their chosen advertisements, analyses of the advertisements, changes they had made in order to subvert the advertisements, and their intended messages. Students then discussed how well the intended messages were communicated.

One student, Maria (pseudonym), subverted a Canadian Goose advertisement. This advertisement displays a person in a Canadian Goose coat walking through the snow away from a helicopter (suggesting a remote place). Maria discussed that the advertisement was promoting the warmth and durability of the garments the company sells. As a vegan who conscientiously researches into how companies use and treat animals, Maria knew many companies like this one will pluck the feathers from geese while they are living, allow the feathers to grow back, and then pluck them again in a vicious cycle of abuse for the animals. She created her own subvertisement in response.

She chose to use similar language: where the Canadian Goose advertisement said, "OUTDOOR PERFORMANCE," Maria changed the language to

Figure 8.3.   A subvertisement created by adbusters.org.
Source: Student created.

"INDOOR Performance," drawing attention to what goes on inside the factory as well as what is inside the garment that Canadian Goose is selling.

The image is completely different: the original displays someone wearing a coat outside, in a snowy terrain, a helicopter in the background; Maria's image shows a person's legs in shorts—indicating that the person is indoors—splayed on either side of a goose. One hand holds the goose by the neck and the other pulls feathers off the body, half of which has been plucked naked. Causing the reader to look into the making of the garment by juxtaposing her image with the original advertisement, Maria applies irony, as she and her classmates had discussed in class.

Responding to Texts: Creating Remixes and Mashups

In a previous high school English course, Steffany taught students who were mostly white about the school to prison pipeline with the novel *To Kill a Mockingbird*. During this unit, she and her students examined four issues within the novel that contribute to the school to prison pipeline: single-parent homes, lynching and racial discrimination, the criminal justice system, and poverty.

After they examined the novel and other important texts—Walter Dean Myers's (2004) YA screenplay *Monster*, informational texts on each issue, articles on the Mississippi Burning trial, portions of PBS's *Eyes on the Prize* miniseries, popular films, photographs of lynching and people living in poverty, and even songs—she asked students to consider critical questions they had been asking throughout the unit in their reading journals and in class, and then to determine an issue they wanted to explore further.

Students researched their issues and then created a written piece as well as a mashup or remix that they presented to the class. Dan (pseudonym) researched into America's criminal justice system, finding further evidence of racial discrimination. For his presentation, he remixed a commercial for a prominent lawyer in his state, dubbing portions of it with his own satirical recordings that addressed disparities between legal representation for white people and for people of color, especially those who cannot afford to pay for legal representation.

Dan edited his piece on iMovie, but there are several other technological tools that can perform similar functions, such as Animoto. Animoto is a

Figure 8.4. A Canadian Goose advertisement.

Figure 8.5. A subvertisement created by a student.
Source: **Student created.**

website where students can create thirty-second videos for free. Educators can get free subscriptions, which allow them to register up to fifty students who can create videos of any length. If a teacher wanted more than fifty students to have access, there is an annual fee of $30 (www.animoto.com).

During the portion of this unit focused on lynching and racial discrimination, Steffany showed her students postcards with images of lynching in America that collector James Allen has compiled into a website: www. withoutsanctuary.org. She also showed them Depression-era photographs when they were discussing poverty within the novel's timeframe. Another possible assignment for students would be to create mashups with some of these photographs and modern-day photographs, creating a piece that is saying something new.

Hope (pseudonym) created a mashup with her poem—written about poverty in America—set to Depression-era photographs, and set the slide show to music, effectively creating the desired mood for her piece (posted on YouTube: https://www.youtube.com/watch?v=d3euOVmtjik).

Poverty is an underlying issue in *To Kill a Mockingbird*, but through her project and presentation, Hope drew it out in insightful ways. While her piece was powerful, Steffany determined that if a student were to create something like this again, she would suggest that they mash it up with some contemporary images of poverty along with those from the 1930s. A piece like this would communicate a different message, moving the audience toward thinking about history in conjunction with the present day.

Hope created her presentation on Windows Movie Maker, but students could also use technology like Voicethread to create similar presentations.

Voicethread allows users to create slides with pictures, video, graphics, and web links, and students can add their own voices to the presentation (www.voicethread.com). Thus, a presentation can play on its own with the narrative power of the creator's voice.

If a school has iPads for student use, an app with similar features is Shadow Puppet (available through iTunes). This app provides opportunity for students to combine photos and video clips with their own voice recording and any song. Students can also draw on the screen, add emojis, zoom in, and pan out for effect (www.get-puppet.co/).

If ELA teachers wanted to further explore poverty, they could pair this text with a beautiful YA novel that addresses childhood poverty: Rowell's *Eleanor & Park*. This novel, set in the 1980s, focuses on that decade's pop culture, especially music. Park and Eleanor meet on the school bus on Eleanor's first day at a new school, bond through music and comics, and eventually fall in love.

The contrast between Park's home life and Eleanor's is stark: Park's parents love each other, and they live in a nice, middle-class home. Eleanor's mother, due at least in part to her economic situation, lives with an abusive man, and Eleanor and all her brothers and sisters—who have to share one small bedroom—live in fear of him. Eleanor has few things she can call her own, and she works hard every day to put together an outfit to wear to school.

Figure 8.6. A postcard. Part of James Allen's collection in *Without Sanctuary: Lynching Photography in America*.

Focusing on Eleanor's situation, students in Steffany's introduction to literature course explored the issue of childhood poverty. She first asked students to research into childhood poverty. Students came to class with statistics like this: in 2000, 16.1 percent of U.S. children lived in poverty. In 2008, that number grew to 18.9 percent. That is, fourteen million children (Wight, Chau, Thampi, and Aratani, 2010). Students shared their research, and then the class discussed questions like, "What does it mean for a child to live in poverty?" and "What kind of control do they have over their lives?"

Teachers who would like to continue this examination of poverty could study images of childhood poverty in the world today, connecting them to the photographs examined while reading *To Kill a Mockingbird*. Then, after students have read, discussed, questioned, and researched the issue, they could create mashups modeled after *Without Sanctuary* postcards. While using images of sweatshops, or of absurdly rich mansions mashed up with images of poverty, they could add satirical comments: "Wish you were here!" or "Having fun!" Perhaps students could also promote awareness by moving the project into the rest of the school.

BEYOND THE CLASSROOM: PUBLICATION, SERVICE LEARNING, AND ADVOCACY

By posting writings, projects, and presentations in public spaces, students are creating for an audience much wider than just the teacher or even their own classroom peers. This may prompt students to carefully plan and execute their projects, paying close attention to the finishing touches before posting them in public or online. Several of Steffany's students posted their final projects on YouTube, but if students were creating a campaign, they could develop their own website or a page on the teacher's website.

When students are working for a cause important to them, the desire to create polished, effective pieces is further enhanced. An exciting way to end this unit would be to have students organize service learning projects, where they are working to make a difference in their community. Groups could partner with local organizations working toward ending the cycle of poverty, and thus students' awareness and empathy could turn to advocacy.

CREATING A PARTICIPATORY CULTURE

While this paints a portrait of critical inquiry in the author's classroom, this approach to teaching can take shape in many different forms. When combined with a cultural studies approach, critical inquiry allows students to draw upon multiple texts—literature, informational text, film, popular culture, news articles, and social media—both to pose their questions and to search for answers.

In this way, asking questions and seeking answers becomes a recursive process. Students pose questions based on what they are reading and consuming from all the sources available to them, and when they find answers to their questions, these answers can pose further questions, encouraging students to continue to explore (Beach, Thein, and Webb, 2016, 6). Teachers like Katie, Jenny, and Jamie foster this kind of recursive learning in their classrooms.

Katie teaches eighth-grade ELA in an urban junior high school in Michigan. Her students read YAL all year, in whole-class reads, book clubs, and independent reading. By April, students have learned how book clubs are structured, following the Harvey and Daniels model (2009). For the year's last book club project, students select from culturally diverse historical fiction: *My Name Is Not Easy* by Edwardson, *A Long Walk to Water* by Park, *The Surrender Tree* by Engle, *Far from Home* by Robert, *Climbing the Stairs* by Venkatraman, and *Never Fall Down* by McCormick. Groups form by book choice and not by reading level (Harvey and Daniels, 2009).

While students read and discuss in their book clubs, they employ critical inquiry through questioning, inferring, and making connections surrounding issues inherent in the texts. They also read informational texts related to these issues. In groups, students discuss the issues of their inquiry throughout their reading. Deciding on one issue to explore further, they research this issue, write a "We-search" paper (think "I-search" for groups) collaboratively through Google Docs, and then create a remix presentation complete with images, video, and audio components. The culminating piece is the group presentations.

Through book clubs and inquiry circles, Katie has created a "participatory culture" in her classroom (Jenkins, 2006). Henry Jenkins defines "participatory culture" as one in which students are allowed to express themselves artistically, discuss important issues with one another, share their creations, and engage in "informal mentorship" (2006).

Engaging in critical inquiry through book clubs, inquiry circles, and their collaborative writing and remix creation, students research, think critically, discuss, create, mentor, connect, and teach. Collaborative writing is a valid activity to teach in ELA classrooms, and remixes and mashups invite student collaboration. Wikis are a great space for collaborative writing, as are Google Docs and many other Web 2.0 tools.

Jenny and Jamie also create participatory cultures in their classrooms. These seventh-grade teachers team up for a unit on World War II in their rural Michigan middle school. Jenny teaches ELA; Jamie, social studies. Throughout this unit, students read critically, inquire into issues in their novels, research and write collaboratively, create multimodal presentations, and teach their peers. Additionally, these students publish their work beyond the classroom: on Wikipedia.

UTILIZING WIKIPEDIA IN THE CLASSROOM

Thus, Jamie's students are using a tool that is most often utilized for research, and one that is sometimes viewed with scorn. Because Wikipedia pages can be created by anyone, teachers may ask students to completely avoid the site or to use it only as a launching pad for more reputable websites. Wikipedia pages are highly monitored, though, and are often revised if false information is published on a page. Still, because faulty information *can* be included, there is a risk of students gathering flawed research. However, Jamie has decided to use Wikipedia's system to her (and her students') advantage.

For their World War II unit, Jenny and Jamie teach with a critical inquiry, cultural studies approach. In both their social studies and ELA classes, students read and discuss informational texts and historical documents related to World War II. In addition to these texts, they are also viewing film, listening to podcasts, and perusing websites devoted to World War II. In Jenny's ELA classes, the students choose from several YA historical fiction texts about World War II, form literature circles based on their choices, and read the texts, discussing them with the students in their literature circles (Harvey and Daniels, 2009).

While reading these YA books, students are questioning, wondering, and responding critically in their reading journals. Once they finish their books and their reading in social studies, students choose an issue. In inquiry circles, they research their issue in both their social studies and ELA classes. In social studies, their group creates a Wikipedia page in which they disseminate their research. Thus, they use Wikipedia's unique publication policy as a platform, adding their voices to those who have published there before. Then, in their ELA classes, they create multimodal presentations and teach peers about their topic.

MULTIMODAL PRESENTATIONS: TEACHING
PEERS AND OTHERS

Multimodal presentations are exciting ways for students to share their learning with peers in their classrooms, but they could also share these with a wider audience. Glogster is one tool teachers can use with their students that makes creating presentations and digital storytelling simple. With Glogster (or eduGlogster for educators), students can arrange pictures, videos, text, clip art, and web links into a digital "poster" in order to present their story or research project to the class. Thus, Glogster is the perfect tool for remix and mashup projects.

These posters are creative ways to display information, and when students present, they can move through each element on their poster, guiding their audience in the order they would like them to go. The poster provides an attractive, condensed space to contain information, and each textbox has a scroll bar, so there could be more information within that textbox than what is immediately visible. If a teacher would like students to publish to a wider audience than their classroom, students can make their posters public on the Glogster website (www.edu.glogster.com).

Glogster would be an excellent tool for students to share their *Eleanor & Park* and *To Kill a Mockingbird* mashups while also connecting research they have found on childhood poverty and writing they have done on that research. If students formed service learning groups, they could include photos and videos of their service learning in the Glogster poster and then publish their posters on the teacher's or school's website.

CONCLUSION

There are so many exciting opportunities for ELA students to learn and grow through reading and responding to YAL by mashing up a critical inquiry approach and effective use of technology. While incorporating technology into the classroom engages students, educators also need to promote the examination of textual content and its connection to important societal and cultural issues. Through critical reading and thinking, and analyzing and creating remixes and mashups, students are engaged in activities and learning that help to develop them into critically thinking, change-making citizens in a diverse and developing society.

REFERENCES

Allen, J., ed. 2000. *Without sanctuary: Lynching photography in America.* Santa Fe, NM: Twin Palms Publishers.

Anderson, M. T. 2012. *Feed.* Cambridge, MA: Candlewick Press.

Beach, R., A. H. Thein, and A. Webb. 2016. *Teaching to Exceed the English Language Arts Common Core State Standards,* 2nd ed. New York: Routledge.

Campbell, H. A. 2000. "Thinner than ever." *Adbusters.* http://www.adbusters.org/spoofads/ad-game/.

Elliot-Johns, S. 2012. "Literacy Teacher Education Today and the Teaching of Adolescent Literature." In *Teaching Young Adult Literature Today: Insights, Considerations, and Perspectives for the Classroom Teacher,* edited by J. Hayn and J. Kaplan. Lanham, MD: Rowman & Littlefield.

Foucault, M. 1990. *The History of Sexuality: An Introduction.* Vol. 1. Translated by R. Hurley. New York: Vintage.

Freire, P. 2000. *Pedagogy of the Oppressed.* New York: Continuum.

Giroux, H. A. 2010. "Lessons from Paulo Freire." *The Chronicle of Higher Education.*

Hampton, H., director. 2000. *Eyes on the Prize: America's Civil Rights Years 1954–1965* [Miniseries]. USA: PBS.

Harvey, S., and H. Daniels. 2009. *Comprehension and Collaboration: Inquiry Circles in Action.* Portsmouth, NH: Heinemann.

Horkheimer, M. 1982. *Critical Theory Selected Essays.* New York: Continuum.

Jenkins, H. 2006. "Confronting the Challenges of Participatory Culture: Media Education for the 21st Century." In *Confessions of an Aca-Fan: The Official Weblog of Henry Jenkins.* Retrieved from http://henryjenkinds.org/2006/10/confronting_the_challenges_of.html.

Lee, H. 1988. *To Kill a Mockingbird.* New York: Grand Central Publishing.

Merriam-Webster. 2017. "Meme." https://www.merriam-webster.com/dictionary/meme.

Myers, W. D. 2004. *Monster.* New York: HarperCollins.

Pope, R. 1995. *Textual Intervention: Critical and Creative Strategies for Literary Studies.* New York: Routledge.

Rowell, R. 2013. *Eleanor & Park.* New York: St. Martin's Griffin.

Santaella, L. 1997. "The Development of Peirce's Three Types of Reasoning: Abduction, Deduction, and Induction." *6th Congress of the IASS.*

Wight, V., M. Chau, K. Thampi, and Y. Aratani. 2010. "Childhood Poverty and the Social Safety Net: Examining the Landscape of Child Poverty in the US Today." *Current Problems in Pediatric and Adolescent Health Care* 40 (10): 263–266.

Index

About the Editors

Steven T. Bickmore is associate professor of English education in the Department of Teaching and Learning in the College of Education at the University of Nevada, Las Vegas (UNLV). He taught high school English in the Jordan School District in the Salt Lake City area from 1980 to 2008. In addition to teaching English courses, including Advanced Placement courses, he taught Latin and humanities. His many teacher awards and recognitions included an NEH/Reader's Digest Teacher Scholar Award (a full-year paid research sabbatical) for the 1989–1990 school year, and he was a winner of the prestigious Milken Educator Award in 1999. He is a cofounder and coeditor of *Study and Scrutiny: Research in Young Adult Literature*. Bickmore began his university teaching at Louisiana State University in 2008 before moving to UNLV in 2015. He has authored or coauthored over thirty academic papers and book chapters and published in a variety of journals.

Jennifer S. Dail is associate professor of English education in the Department of English at Kennesaw State University in Kennesaw, Georgia. She also directs the Kennesaw Mountain Writing Project (KMWP), a National Writing Project site serving teachers Pre-K through college in all content areas. She has received multiple grant awards supporting the work of KMWP, including an Improving Teacher Quality grant. Prior to joining the faculty at Kennesaw State University in 2006, she taught English education courses at the University of Alabama and taught middle and high school English. Dail served as coeditor of *SIGNAL Journal*, International Reading Association's journal, focusing on young adult literature, from 2008 to 2013. She is also an active member of several educational organizations, including the National Council of Teachers of English (NCTE) and the National Writing Project (NWP). She serves on the board for the Georgia Council of Teachers of English as the interim conference director and college liaison. Dail has published multiple articles on young adult literature and technology in *The ALAN Review* and has several book chapters focusing on this work as well.

Shelbie Witte is the Kim and Chuck Watson Chair in Education and associate professor of adolescent literacy and English education at Oklahoma State University, where she directs the Oklahoma State University Writing Project and leads the Initiative for 21st Century Literacies Research. Her research focuses on the intersection of twenty-first-century literacies and pedagogy, particularly at the middle level. She is coeditor, along with Sara Kajder, of NCTE's *Voices from the Middle.*About the Contributors

About the Contributors

Kathryn Bailey is a secondary English teacher in the Henry County School System, currently teaching at Hampton High School in Hampton, Georgia. She received her undergraduate and graduate degrees in secondary English education from Kennesaw State University in Kennesaw, Georgia.

Crystal L. Beach is a high school English teacher and a doctoral candidate at the University of Georgia in the Department of Language and Literacy Education. Her interests include new literacies, identity, multimodalities, popular culture, and technologies in the secondary English classroom. She writes about these topics to offer educators ways to consider how they might create a more meaningful pedagogy for their unique students. Currently, she is working on a project that focuses on sports literacies and representations of female athletes' bodies.

Kate Bedard currently teaches English at Bassick High School in Bridgeport, Connecticut, where she advocates for urban youth, storytelling, and creativity.

Mike P. Cook is assistant professor at Auburn University, where he teaches undergraduate and graduate courses within the English education program. He utilizes comics and graphic novels in his preparation of preservice and graduate-level ELA teachers and has done research, presented, and published on using graphic novels to foster engagement, comprehension, and multimodal literacy. His scholarship has appeared in *SIGNAL Journal*, *Sequential Art Narrative in Education*, and the *Journal of College Literacy and Learning*, among others.

Bryan Ripley Crandall, PhD, is director of the Connecticut Writing Project at Fairfield University (CWP-Fairfield) and assistant professor of literacy in the Graduate School of Education and Allied Professions. His interests include writing instruction, young adult literature, refugee and immigrant youth, and community-based scholarship.

Michelle M. Falter is a former middle and high school English teacher and is currently assistant professor of English education at North Carolina State University. Her scholarship focuses on English teacher education; young adult literature; emotion in the teaching of literature and writing in the secondary classroom; and participatory, dialogic, and critical, feminist pedagogies that help educators co-construct knowledge with their students. She is also the coeditor of the book *Teaching outside the Box but inside the Standards: Making Room for Dialogue* (2016), with Bob Fecho and Xiaoli Hong.

Paula Fortuna teaches world literature at the Center for Global Studies in Norwalk, Connecticut. Her students explore their place in the world through the processes of analyzing and creating a wide variety of texts. As a world traveler herself, she celebrates diversity, multiculturalism, perspectives, and international integrity. She is a teacher-fellow of CWP-Fairfield.

Kim Herzog teaches English at Staples High School in Westport, Connecticut. She is the faculty advisor of award-winning literary magazines and is the teacher-leader of her school's technological efforts. In 2015–2016, she was her district's Teacher of the Year and was a state semifinalist for Connecticut Teacher of the Year.

Breanne Huston is a PhD candidate at the University of Georgia and a full-time high school English teacher. She also works closely with the Red Clay Writing Project, a local site of NWP.

Steffany Comfort Maher is a doctoral candidate in English education at Western Michigan University and is currently writing her dissertation on critical inquiry approaches to teaching young adult literature. Her research interests include intersections between cultural studies, critical youth studies, young adult literature, and preservice teacher education. The mother of four daughters, Steffany is also interested in the reading practices of "adolescent" girls. In addition to her chapter in this book, she has published an article in *English Journal* entitled "Using *To Kill a Mockingbird* as a Conduit for Teaching about the School-to-Prison Pipeline."

Shaun Mitchell teaches African-American literature, playwriting, and Advanced Placement literature at Central High School in Bridgeport,

Connecticut. When he is not teaching in the classroom, he directs and advises the Central Players, the drama program at his school. In 2016, he was a finalist for Connecticut Teacher of the Year. Shaun also is a lead instructor of several of the Young Adult Literacy Labs offered through CWP-Fairfield.

Rikki Roccanti Overstreet is a doctoral candidate in curriculum and instruction with an emphasis in English education at Florida State University. With a master's degree in post-1900 literary and cultural studies, she is interested in how literature and literacy evolve with time, technology, politics, and culture, and how such changes shape adolescent readers and affect the ELA classroom. In conjunction with this interest, she studies young adult literature, transmedia stories, and twenty-first-century literacies.

Lesley Roessing taught middle school for twenty years. She now serves as founding director of the Coastal Savannah Writing Project and senior lecturer in the College of Education at Armstrong State University. Lesley is the author of several professional books for teachers including *The Write to Read: Response Journals That Increase Comprehension, Comma Quest: The Rules They Followed—The Sentences They Saved, No More "Us" and "Them": Classroom Lessons & Activities to Promote Peer Respect,* and *Bridging the Gap: Reading Critically and Writing Meaningfully to Get to the Core,* as well as articles for NCTE, NWP, ELMLE, and AMLE publications. She is also a columnist for *AMLE Magazine.*

Leslie Rush is associate dean of undergraduate programs and director in the School of Teacher Education at the University of Wyoming.

Brandon L. Sams is assistant professor of English at Iowa State University. He is interested in pedagogies of identity development in preservice teacher education, the role of critical reflection in developing and maintaining culturally sustaining classrooms, and contemplative literature and writing pedagogy.

Jennifer von Wahlde teaches English at Darien High School in Connecticut and is a part-time communications instructor for Post University. Her passion for teaching is rooted in fostering creative expression and growth opportunities for her students. She is a teacher-fellow who instructs in CWP-Fairfield's Young Adult Literacy Labs.

Julie Warner is a former high school teacher and holds National Board Teaching Certification. She has a decade of experience implementing professional development for teachers across grade levels and subject areas in technology and literacy. She has also worked as a K–12 education policy advisor in the U.S. Senate and as an education research analyst at the U.S. Department of Education. Prior to her federal service, Julie taught university faculty teaching courses in writing, linguistics, and Internet ethics. She also served as technology director of the Coastal Savannah Writing Project. She is the author of *Adolescents' New Literacies with and through Mobile Phones* as well as articles for the *Journal of Literacy Research* and *SIGNAL Journal*.

Megan Zabilansky is an English teacher at Joel Barlow High School in Redding, Connecticut. She currently teaches AP Language and Composition, Writing to Speak: Words to Be Heard, and sophomore and junior general English. She is also a teacher-fellow of the CWP-Fairfield.